The Awakening

THE AWAKENING:

The Seawright-Ellison Family Saga, Vol. 1
A Narrative History

BY WALTER B. CURRY, JR., ED. D

PALMETTO
PUBLISHING

Charleston, SC
www.PalmettoPublishing.com

The Awakening

First Edition

ISBN: 978-1-63837-282-0

BOOK DEDICATIONS

This book is dedicated to the memory of my cousin, Otis A. Corbitt, who birthed the vision of this book through years of genealogical knowledge and the desire to unite two families who share a common ancestor.

Otis A. Corbitt, Ph. D.
Son of John & Thelma Ellison Corbitt

To the memory of my grandparents, Wallace & Armenia Wooden Seawright, my uncles Wallace & Roosevelt Seawright, my aunts Barbra Seawright Garvin and Wanda McKie Seawright, my first cousin Lakeshia Seawright, my great uncle Wilson Seawright, my great aunt Catherine Seawright, cousins Bobby Seawright, Sandy Sessoms, Roosevelt Seawright of Aiken, SC, Henry Seawright, Mildred Seawright Patterson, Tommy Ellison, James "Shot" Brown, Floster L. Ellison, Jr., James "Bud Ellison, Jr., Thaddeus Ellison, Travis Hall, Joseph "Bubba" Seawright, Keidre J. Corbett, MD.

Special dedications to my wife, Takiyah S. Curry, and our handsome sons, Braxton and Braylon Curry. The family of Wallace & Armenia Wooden Seawright: my mother Cheryl S. Seawright, my aunts and uncles, my first cousins, second cousins, third cousins. My great aunt, Nancy Johnson Seawright. To all the descendants of my great-grandparents, Robert L. & Alice Thompson Seawright, Romeo Ellison, Louise Jenkins Seawright, The Ellison-Miles Family Council, Martha Ellison Oliver, Martha Seawright Minor, Wendell Miles, and John H. Corbitt, Sr.

CONTENTS

PREFACE

When my grandparents, Wallace and Armenia Wooden Seawright, Sr. died over twenty-five years ago, my mother, Cheryl Seawright Curry, and her siblings faced difficult challenges. In mourning the death of their parents, they were very young in age; the oldest sibling was thirty-seven, and the youngest sibling was thirteen. Some of the siblings had to become surrogate parents to the younger siblings, and some siblings had to raised themselves. Without the presence their parents, my mother and her siblings had to learn to live without them.

A few years passed after the death of my grandfather; the contact between his siblings and my mother and her siblings were limited. My grandfather's brother, Wilson Seawright, never returned home to visit. However, my grandfather's sister, Catherine Seawright McCollough, along with her husband, Jackson "Jaycee" McCullough, returned home and stayed for a few years in the early 1990s. When I became a teenager and began to drive, I visited them very often. During the visits, my great aunt with me stories about the family like my mother. She revealed that my great-great-grandfather's name is Arthur Seawright! I was shocked to hear that my uncle was named after him! She shared with me another revelation: there was another relative named Roosevelt Seawright who lived in Aiken! Although I knew my uncle and my second cousin named "Roosevelt Seawright," another relative with the same name shocked me! I immediately asked her for his contact information, and she obliged. When I contacted Cousin Roosevelt, he shared another revelation! He said that his father's name is Wilson Seawright! I could not believe there was another relative who had the same name as my great uncle! He also stated that he had an old family Bible he wanted me to see. Unfortunately, I never had a chance to read it.

While I gleaned information from Cousin Roosevelt, he suggested that I reach out to another relative, Otis Corbitt, who lived in Columbia. When I first contacted Otis, he shared with me a wealth of information. During our conservations and frequent visits, more revelations were revealed! Through him, I found out that I am related to several relatives who were trailblazers: The "Superstar of Gospel," Tommy Ellison, a legendary pioneer in African American gospel music, and Floster T. Ellison, Jr., who founded the Palmetto Barber Association in 1960. I had the distinctive pleasure to meet them and continued contact until their passing. Otis also invited me to the Ellison-Miles Family Reunion in 1999, where I met more relatives, including my great-grandfather first cousins, Romeo Ellison and Martha Ellison Oliver, and learned more about the family. I was excited because, before that time, I had never attended a family reunion.

In conjunction with my research about the Ellison family, I continued to do research and extend my relationships in the Seawright family. Around 1998, I reached out to my great aunt, Nancy J. Seawright.[1] A kind and generous woman by nature, Aunt Nancy has shared many stories about my grandparents, my grandfather's siblings, my great-grandparents, and other relatives. No doubt, her accounts have provided me a knowledge base to dig deeper about the family. Over the years, I have consulted other relatives who have shared information with me.

The epiphany moment for me to write an account about the family was upon the passing of my cousin, Otis Corbitt, on September 6, 2009. Otis was known to everyone in the family, as well as to other African American families in the Wagener-Salley area, for being astute in family history. Before his passing, he instructed me to begin writing a family history book. He said he did not have much time to live and the future of our efforts rested on my shoulders. I agreed.

The expansiveness of knowledge has inspired me to write a collection of narratives in a book series called, *The Awakening: The Seawright-Ellison Family Saga, Vol. 1, A Narrative History*. The book is the first volume of narratives about the descendants of two families who share a common ancestor, Martha Kitchings Seawright Ellison. The family saga begins with Martha and her family, who were sharecroppers who lived and worked on the Hugh E. Phillips plantation near Williston, South Carolina, during the Reconstruction Era, and the circumstances that involved her marriages to Dave Seawright, Sr. and Joseph Ellison, Sr. The saga continues with contextualized resurrected stories of relatives who were forgotten over the years.

The Seawright narratives include the stories of Robert L. Seawright, who charismatically and jovially survived the challenges of life despite his shortcomings and untimely the deaths of his young parents. The story of Robert's son, Wallace Seawright, Sr., a beloved husband, father, deacon at Baughmanville Baptist Church, Prince Hall Mason, and sharecropper, raised his family

---

1   Nancy J. Seawright is the wife of Wilson Seawright, son of Robert L. and Alice Thompson Seawright.

of sixteen children with clear moral values and supplemented his income, which allowed him to survive the pitfalls of sharecropping life. The story of two brothers, Roosevelt and Henry Seawright, beloved husbands and fathers, ascended to legendary status, skillfully in brick masonry and craftsmanship in the city of Aiken, South Carolina, and surrounding areas.

The Ellison narratives include the stories of Floster and Nora Miles Ellison, Sr., who were generational pillars of their community through service in their respective professions, families, and roles as deacon and deaconess respectively at Smyrna Missionary Baptist Church. Floster and Nora's son, Floster L. Ellison, Jr., who excelled in professional barbering and social work, inspired by the collective activism during the Civil Rights Movement, co-founded the Palmetto State Barber Association and enjoyed a legendary career as Chief of Social services at Crafts-Farrow State Hospital, an agency of the South Carolina Department of Mental Health. The story of Floster and Nora grandson's, Tommy Ellison, whose experiences as a youth singing on the children choir at Smyrna Missionary Baptist Church, inspired him to pursue a legendary career in African American gospel music, affectionately known by many of his fans as "Mr. Superstar of Gospel."

Research Methods

The objective in gathering information was to document the narratives through written historical data, personal experiences, and interviews—oral and written—with those who were familiar with the individuals in this book. The contents of this book are aligned with the Genealogical Proof Standard (GPS) ascribed by the Board for Certification of Genealogists. The constituents of the standard ensure that family histories are accurate and reflect historical reality as closely as possible. Secondary sources were consulted as well.

Organization of the Book

The body of the book is organized into chapter biographies of unique individuals of the Seawright-Ellison family, chosen on based on the litany of archived information. The appendices consist of documentation (pictures, primary sources, etc.) and other pertinent information.

Through Slavery and War in South Carolina, through Reconstruction Era and Beyond: The Story of Martha Kitchings Seawright Ellison

"I am what time, circumstance, history, have made of me, certainly, but I am also, much more than that. So are we all"—James Baldwin

Martha Kitchings, the daughter of Samuel and Becky Kitchings, was born enslaved on November 20, 1849, in Barnwell District, South Carolina.[2] Her parents' origins are unknown. According to legend, the family was enslaved by the Kitchings family, who were white and lived near the area known as the Skillet Community in between Salley and Aiken, South Carolina.[3] Martha had nine siblings: Furman Kitchings, Wheeler Kitchings, John Kitchings, Peter Kitchngs, Henry Kitchings, Pasha Kitchings, Mary Kitchings, Sarah Kitchings, and Ellen Kitchings.

During the time of Martha's birth, Barnwell District had an agricultural economy dominated by cotton. The district's abundance of silt loam was prime soil that contained silt and clay suitable for cotton growth.[4] In 1850, Barnwell was the second producing cotton district in the state, be-

---

2 Barnwell District, now Barnwell County, was created in 1798 from the area formerly known as Winton County. Located at the southwestern edge of South Carolina, the district originally encompassed 1,440 square miles but lost most of its territory to the creation of Aiken County (1871), Bamberg County (1897), and Allendale County (1919). The district was named for John Barnwell of Beaufort in recognition of his military service to South Carolina.

3 A philanthropist named Della Kitchings owned over 500 acres of wooded land. She told African Americans, if they cleaned up the land during the first year, she would give them half of what they made. Some balked at the proposition because it was counterintuitive. They warned if African Americans acquiesced Della's proposition, they would be hungry to a point of "licking a biscuit from a skillet."

4 Jenkins, Ellen Bush and Belcher, Posey.Barnwell County. Columbia, SC: University of South Carolina, Institute for Southern Studies, 2016.

hind only Edgefield. Cotton wealth contributed to an increased rise in the local slave population.[5] Whites comprised almost 80 percent of the local population, but in 1850, they were a minority.[6]

Barnwell had several geographical advantages. This district's waterways, including the Savannah, Edisto, and Salkehatchie Rivers and their many tributaries, were abundant sources of timber and lumber for low-country markets. The completion of a railroad from Charleston to Hamburg through the district in 1833 transformed small communities like Williston and Blackville into booming economic centers. The railroad was mainly completed by slaves. These advantages positioned the district to grow economically and attract migrants who sought a better quality of life. Some migrants became plantation owners using enslaved labor.

On December 20, 1860, South Carolina was the first state to secede from the Union. South Carolina, along with seven states, established the Confederate States of America in February 1861. On the early morning of April 12, 1861, Confederate guns opened fire on Fort Sumter near Charleston, South Carolina. This action led to the beginning of the bloodiest war in American history, known as the Civil War. Men from Barnwell District answered the call of duty. The district's men served in the 11th Regiment Reserves of the 43rd Barnwell, Company A; the 2nd Regiment of South Carolina Troops of the 43rd Barnwell, Company E; and other military units.[7] In addition, the state impressed enslaved labor and drafted White men and African American freed males to support the military effort.

In early 1865, the Confederacy was losing the war. The Union's "shock and awe" strategy by destructive means broke the Confederate will to fight. On January 15, 1865, Union general William T. Sherman and his troops crossed the Savannah River into South Carolina. Sherman's objective was to attack the state capital, Columbia. On their way to Columbia, Union troops marched into Barnwell District town of Williston. The town was situated on the main road and railroad between Augusta and the Low Country. The Confederacy transported goods (i.e., food, weapons) and occasionally troops to the Low Country areas. The Union objective was to destroy the railroad tracks and pillage the town. On the night of February 8, 1865, Union troops led by General Judson Kilpatrick burned Williston, and residents were fleeing for their lives.[8] Only a few homes were spared.

---

5   Jenkins and Belcher, Barnwell County.

6   Ibid.

7   Seilger, Robert S. South Carolina's military organizations during the War between the States. Charleston: History Press, 2008.

8   "History-The War Between The States."; retrieved from http://www.williston-sc.com/history/war/.

In 1925, Mary Phillips Harvey's memoir briefly recounts her family's life during and after the Civil War:

My home was in ruins—a mass of brick and ashes. The flower yard trampled by the feet of many horses, and pieces of my piano scattered around. Some kind-hearted soldiers, (for some kind) saved it from the flames, only to be broken in pieces by others. Some even cut the wires out with an axe and gave them to some poor people who lived near us, and the made knitting needles of it.[9]

The war was officially over on April 9, 1865, when Confederate General Robert E. Lee surrendered his army at Appomattox Court House to Union General Ulysses S. Grant. Two months later, on June 19, 1865, Union soldiers, led by Major General Gordon Granger, landed at Galveston, Texas and announced that the war had ended and that the enslaved were now free.[10] Slavery was officially abolished on December 6, 1865, concomitant with the passage of the 13th Amendment.

Martha was sixteen years old when slavery officially ended. Her family, along with other formerly enslaved families transitioned into freedom. As newly freedmen, they had to learn to live as freedmen. Secondly, they had to acquire basic needs without assistance from their former masters. Thirdly, they had to acquire proper education. The dire reality of freedmen led Congress to pass the Freedmen's Bureau Act of 1865.[11] The act created the Freedmen Bureau, which aided and protected freedmen in the South. The bureau was given power to dispense relief to both freedmen and White refugees. The relief included access to medical care, education, and redistribution of abandoned lands to former slaves. The entity was a democratic experiment during the Reconstruction Era (1865–1877), a pivotal time when the country attempted to reunify the divided nation and integrate freedmen into mainstream society.

Although the Freedmen Bureau had some successes, many freedmen were subjugated to systemic racism and economic destitution. In 1865, South Carolina adopted a constitution that made only limited moves toward democracy: instituting the popular election of gubernatorial candidates gubernatorial veto power, and abolishing property qualifications to hold office.[12] Adversely,

9   Harvey, Mary Phillips. Under the Heel of the Invader, ca. 1925., 1925.

10   "Juneteenth Worldwide Celebration." Juneteenth Worldwide Celebration; retrieved from www.juneteenth.com.

11   Schmidt, James D. Freedmen's Bureau. Columbia, SC: University of South Carolina, Institute for Southern Studies, 2016.

12   Graham, Jr., Cole Blease. Constitutions. Columbia, SC: University of South Carolina, Institute for Southern Studies, 2016.

the constitution denied qualified African Americans voting rights and passed the infamous Black Codes to strictly regulate freedmen.[13]

The economic destitution of freedmen was a direct result of a broken promise. Many freedmen hoped that the federal government, through the Freedmen Bureau, would provide them land. The bureau was authorized by law to rent or sell land in its possession to freedmen. Unfortunately, in the summer of 1865, President Andrew Johnson ordered land confiscated by the bureau to be returned to its former owners.[14] The dream of "forty acres and a mule" was dead. Without land, many freedmen had few economic alternatives other than resuming work on plantations owned by former slaveholders, which led to the enacting of the sharecropping system.

Sharecropping was a type of farming in which families rented land from a landowner, in return for a portion of the crop to be given to the landowner at the end of each year. To enact the sharecropping system, freedmen's labor contracts were instituted. Under the direction of the Freedmen Bureau, the contracts consisted of agreements between freedmen laborers and planters, stating terms of employment, such as pay, clothing, housing, and medical care due to the laborers; the part of the crop to be retained by the laborers and the planter; and whether a plot for growing subsistence crops was to be provided. In South Carolina, over 8,000 contracts were signed, and nearly 130,000 freedmen worked under labor contracts between the years 1865 and 1866.[15]

On January 8, 1867, Martha, along with her father and siblings, signed a one-year freedmen labor contract to work for Hugh E. Phillips, a former slaveowner who owned land near Williston, South Carolina. [16] [17] Phillip's wife, Keziah Willis Philips, was the daughter of Williston's founder, Robert Willis. The Phillips family, whose home was destroyed by Sherman's troops during their occupation of Williston, hoped to rebound from their destituion willingly participated in hiring freedmen who were looking for work.[18] The contract stipulated that Phillips agree to furnish housing, land to tend, fuel to burn, and to give the family one third of the crops they grew and gathered. In return, the family must live on the plantation until January 1, 1868, follow directions,

---

13   Graham Jr., Constitutions.

14   Schmidt, James D. Freedmen's Bureau. Columbia, SC: University of South Carolina, Institute for Southern Studies, 2016

15   "Going in Depth ~ SC Freedmen's Bureau Labor Contracts," May 21, 2015; retrieved from https://lowcoun-tryafricana.com/going-in-depth-sc-freedmens-bureau-labor-contracts/.

16   FamilySearch.org "'United States, Freedmen's Bureau Labor Contracts, Indenture and Apprenticeship Records, 1865-1872."

17   Ancesry.com. 1860 U.S Federal Census-Slave Schedule, H.E. Phillips.

18   Harvey, Mary Phillips. Under the Heel of the Invader, ca. 1925., 1925.

and work faithfully. After the family gathered all the crops, they had to pay Phillips out their share for any provisions on anything they bought or got from him.

The labor contract regulated the family to object poverty. Without wages, they had no means to acquire land and materialism that required money. The family was subjugated to the mercy of the landowner. The Black Codes reinstituted the enslavement of former slaves and legally restricted their economic opportunities that yielded income. Furthermore, the circumstances under the sharecropping system made it difficult for the family to progress. Sharecropping life was hard work, full of uncertainties. They had to work constantly to ensure their survival. The inconvenient truth about sharecropping was that the landowner had the most power. Sharecroppers were under constant pressure to perform well for the landowner or face expulsion from the landowner's property. Furthermore, they were in debt to the landowner. Another enormity of sharecropping was that Martha and her family were illiterate, fully illustrated in the 1870 censuses.[19] [20] The illiteracy of the family was riveting which meant that acquisition of literacy was not prioritized, which also included other freedmen laborers and their families. Many children from sharecropping families did not attend school or complete school because of the labor demands that sharecropping placed on their families.

Since there were no political and social protections in place legally, the state did not fully enforce the Civil Rights Act of 1866, which guaranteed all citizens, regardless of race and color, protection of their civil rights, such as the right to file suit, make and enforce contracts, buy and sell, and inherit real and personal property.[21] Although freedmen could file civil rights complaints to the bureau, landowners still had power unless the federal government intervened. Congress eventually disallowed the 1865 constitution and ordered the creation of a new one. Under the authority of the congressional Reconstruction Acts, a state constitution met in Charleston on January 14, 1868.[22] Under federal military supervision, African American men voted in South Carolina for the first time in the election of delegates, and three-fifths of the total were African American.[23] Many whites refused to participate in the ratification election.

---

19   FamilySearch.org. 1870 United States Federal Census.

20   FamilySearch.org.

21   "History, Art & Archives, U.S. House of Representatives, "The Civil Rights Bill of 1866."; retrieved from www.history.house.gov/Historical-Highlights/1851-1900/The-Civil-Rights-Bill-of-1866/.

22   Graham, Cole Blease (2016). Constitutions. Columbia, SC: University of South Carolina, Institute for Southern Studies, 2016.

23   Graham, Constitutions.

Congress ratified **the new constitution** on April 16, 1868.[24] The new constitution remained the only constitution to be submitted directly to the people for approval. Furthermore, the constitution included several democratic reforms, such as free public education regardless of race and women's rights. Pivotally, it abolished the Black Codes that disenfranchised and marginalized African Americans in South Carolina.

The abolishment of the Black Codes also eliminated the labor contract provision that required freedmen laborers not to leave the landowner premises or receive visitors without the landowner permission. As a result, the family was able to travel freely, which afforded opportunities to seek employment elsewhere. The 1870 census record showed that Martha's father and her siblings were no longer employed by Phillips.[25] They relocated to nearby Windsor, a town which is located a few miles west of Williston. The family continued to sharecrop.

Before 1870, Martha decided not to live with her family. She decided to get married and start a family. Between the years of 1868 and 1869, she met and married Dave Seawright. Born a slave in 1844, Dave was previously married to a woman named Mary. They had a son named Dave Seawright, Jr. **Dave** also had a daughter, Mariah Seawright Livingston, from a woman named Lucy Mack. The 1870 census shows that Dave and Martha lived in Tabernacle Township of western Orangeburg County, South Carolina.[26] Their union were blessed with six children: Flora Seawright, Henrietta Seawright Gibson, Armenia Seawright, Curtis "Kirkland" Seawright, Furman Seaw-right, and Arthur Seawright. Occupationally, Dave was a farmer, and Martha was a housekeeper.

On March 10, 1871, African American men Prince Rivers, Charles D. Haynes, Samuel J. Lee, William B. Jones, and others founded Aiken County, which is the only county founded by African Americans in South Carolina, according to records during Reconstruction.[27] The county was named after William Aiken, the first president of the South Carolina Railroad and Canal Company. The county was formed from parts of Barnwell, Lexington, Orangeburg, and Edgefield counties. The Orangeburg County section taken to form Aiken County was northward from the North Edisto River to the south toward Tinker's Creek, where the Seawright family lived since 1870.[28] Therefore, the Seawright family is designated as one of the first families of Aiken County.

---

24 Ibid

25 FamilySearch.org. 1870 United States Federal Census.

26 FamilySearch.org. 1870 United States Federal Census.

27 Cleveland, Christina. "Aiken County Celebrates Founders Day," March 10, 2017. www.aikenstandard.com.

28 "Acts and Joint Resolutions by the Legislature-Sessions 1870 and 1871." The Edgefield Advertiser; retrieved from www.newspapers.com.

On July 4, 1876, the town of Hamburg, a market town mostly populated by African Americans in western Aiken County near Augusta, Georgia, was the center of a key event that was known as the Hamburg Massacre. The massacre was a major civil disturbance that was planned and executed by white Democrats with the goal of suppressing African American voting in the 1876 gubernatorial election. They disrupted Republican meetings and suppressed African American civil rights through violence and intimidation. The massacre resulted in the deaths of four African American men and one white man. About ninety-four white men were indicted, but none were prosecuted. The news of the Hamburg Massacre sent shock waves throughout Aiken County, South Carolina, and nationally.

The 1880 Federal Census record shows that the Seawright family lived in the Rocky Grove Township of Aiken County, where they continued to farm.[29] The township was the settlement for the town of Salley, founded on December 19, 1887, named after Dempsey H. Salley, who was a state legislator responsible for incorporating the town and responsible for the railroad coming through town.[30] The town was formed on a 1,000 acre plantation owned by Salley himself.[31] During the early years, Salley grew progressively with amenities that included naval store manufacturers that produced products from pine resin & lumber, a large hotel, a school, and several local churches.[32] Numerous African American and White families lived in the town and its outskirts. Notable residents included residents who were employees of the Blackville, Alston, and Newberry Railroad Company that came to Salley on December 24, 1887: Jim Keene was an engineer, an African American man named Eli Salley was fireman, Captain W.W. Woodward was conductor, Jack Scott was baggage master, and Pat Donohue was brakeman.[33] In 1876, founded by local African Americans, Sardis Missionary Baptist Church was the first and oldest established church in the town of Salley. In 1925, Sardis School was built for African American children that was designated as an Roenwald School. In 1888, Salley Baptist Church was founded along with the Salley United Methodist Church a few years later.

---

29   Family Search.org. 1880 United States Federal Census.

30   Genealogy Trails History. 90 Years of Aiken County, Aiken County, South Carolina Genealogy Trails; retrieved from www.genealogytrails.com/scar/aiken/aiken_hx.htm.

31   South Carolina Historical Properties Record; retrieved from www.schpr.gov.

32   Genealogy Trails History. 90 Years of Aiken County, Aiken County, South Carolina Genealogy Trails; retrieved from www.genealogytrails.com/scar/aiken/aiken_hx.htm.

33   Genealogy Trails History. 90 Years of Aiken County.

In the early 1880s and 1890s, Aiken County experienced economic challenges.[34] Reconstruction adversely affected businesses that affected local economies. The aftermath of the Civil War required former Confederate states like South Carolina to pay the nation's war debt, pensions to Union Veterans, and pensions to the state's Confederate veterans. Besides this, the Carpetbagger Rule increased the state debt. Railroads destroyed from the war had to be repaired. Schools were closed. Worse, farmers did not have enough money to pay taxes, which resulted in less crop raising and labor shortage.

The economic perils encouraged Aiken County to develop new industries. In the county's eastern section, which included Salley and the new towns of Wagener, Perry, and Seivern, turpentine became a rich resource that created new industries that spurred economic growth. Perry was a bustling center for turpentine dealers.[35] In Wagener, the local newspaper reported that Mr. Manuel Busbee and Mr. Rich bought a turpentine distillery.[36] Furthermore, the local newspaper reported a finding in New Zealand about Kauri gum formed from turpentine as a strategic promotion to incite public interest.[37]

The turpentine industry boom in the eastern Aiken County area opened employment opportunities that attracted people to migrate there. A debonair freedman from Bennettsville, South Carolina, named Joseph Ellison Sr., relocated to Salley. He was employed as a pine tree surveyor for a local turpentine company.[38] Local landowners and businesses were involved in the turpentine industry knew that pine trees had to be surveyed to determine which trees had to be retained or removed. Pine tree surveyors like Joseph were in high demand.

Although the circumstances are unknown, Joseph and Martha courted each other between 1880 and 1886. On October 1, 1886, their oldest son, Floster "Tan" Ellison, Sr., was born. In 1890, Joseph and Martha were married. Martha was fourteen years older than Joseph during the time of their marriage.[39] Besides their son Floster, they had additional children: Joseph D. Ellison, Jr., Jerome "Dune" Ellison, Clinton Ellison, Bessie Ellison, and Oswald Ellison.

The 1900 census shows that the Ellison family were sharecroppers who lived in Tabernacle Township in Aiken County. They settled in the Rustin community located between Salley and Aiken and attended Smyrna Missionary Baptist Church, a prominent African American church

---

34   Genealogy Trails History.

35   "Items for Perry." Aiken Standard, January 11th, 1893; retrieved from www.newspapers.com.

36   "Wagener Wavelets." Aiken Standard, February 17th, 1892; retrieved from www.newspapers.com.

37   "Where Kauri Gum Is Found." Aiken Standard, March 15, 1893; retrieved from www.newspapers.com.

38   Martha E Oliver. "Family History." New York, n.d.

39   Family Search.org. 1900 United States Federal Census.

founded by former slaves in 1871, located near Springfield, South Carolina. In 1913, Joseph and Martha took the responsibility of raising their granddaughter, Mattie Seawright.[40] Later, the family purchased land in the area.[41] On November 10, 1924, nine days after her birthday, Martha died at the old age of seventy-six, due to paralysis.[42] She is remembered as immensely proud, distinguished, and debonair. Four years later, on December 17, 1928, Joseph died at the age of sixty-five, due to pneumonia.[43]

The circumstances involving Martha's first marriage to Dave are shrouded in mystery. I found a death certificate of a "David Searight."[44] According to the document, David died on September 14, 1925, at the age of sixty-eight. He lived in Giddy Swamp township north of Wagener. I noticed that the document confirmed he was married and buried at Smyrna Missionary Baptist Church. There is little evidence to determine whether this David was Martha's first husband based on his age which is a huge gap based on the actual age of Dave, who was twenty-four when he married Martha as noted in the 1870 census. .

Another revelation is Martha's parents. Martha's mother, Becky, is not mentioned in the freedmen labor contract and census records. Did she die, or was she sold away from her family during slavery? Did she die during the Reconstruction era prior to Martha's famiy's signing of the labor contract? Nevertheless, the unsung hero is Martha's father, Sam. During the perilous times of slavery and the Reconstruction era, Sam kept the family together with unwavering commitment and sacrifice. As a single father, he was able to raise his children. Sam's devotion to his family made it possible for the generational procreation of the Kitchings family.

40   Family Search org. 1920 United States Federal Census.

41   Martha E Oliver. "Family History." New York, n.d.

42   Family Search.org. Death Certificate for Martha Ellison.

43   Joseph and Martha Ellison are buried next to each other at Smyrna Missionary Baptist Church, Springfield, South Carolina.

44   Family Search.org. Death Certificate for David Searight.

Despite Shortcomings, Defined by Joviality and Grittiness: The Story of Robert Lee Seawright

"Considering all that's happened in my life, I feel like I'm a pretty levelheaded person that has remained happy and not let my shortcomings overtake the better part of me. I'm fulfilling the things I wanted to fulfill, and I'm still sane"—Leonardo DiCaprio.

"Grandaddy was Grandaddy."—Barbara Seawright Garvin

Robert Lee Seawright, the oldest child of Arthur and Anna Johnson Seawright, was born on September 10, 1903, in the Kitchings Mill community, near Salley, South Carolina.[45] He was the oldest of four siblings: Gadsden Seawright, Mattie Seawright Riley, Annie Mae Seawright Doby, and Gertie Seawright Bennett.[46] [47] [48] [49] [50] [51] [52]

---

45   Ancestry.com. United States World War II Draft Cards Young Men, 1940-1947.

46   Ancestry.com. South Carolina, County Marriage Records, 1907-2000.

47   Ancestry.com. South Carolina, County Marriage Records, 1907-2000.

48   Annie Mae Seawright married David Doby of Williston, SC. Their date of marriage was January 23, 1928. At the time of their marriage, Annie was 18 and David was 21. They were married at Barnwell County Courthouse, Barnwell, SC by J.K. Snelling, Justice of the Peace of Barnwell County. They resided in Williston, SC.

49   Gertie Seawright married Jesse Bennett of Eutawville, SC. Their date of marriage was December 22, 1928. At the time of their marriage, Jesse was 21 and Gertie was 20. They were married at Barnwell County Courthouse, Barnwell, SC by J.K. Snelling, Justice of the Peace of Barnwell County. They resided in Williston, SC.

50   Mattie Seawright married Benjamin Riley. They had one son, Arthur Riley. Arthur died at age of 1.

51   Family Search.org. 1910 United States Federal Census.

52   According to the 1910 census, Robert parents were married since 1902.

Little is known about Robert's parents. According to the 1910 Census, Robert's father was a tenant farmer and earned income from a variety of sources, and his mother too was a farmer and earned wages.[53] On January 11, 1911, Robert's father died at the age of thirty.[54] A few years later, his mother died in her late twenties or early thirties.[55] After the death of his mother, Robert and his siblings were in the care of their paternal and maternal families.[56][57][58] He and his brother, Gadsden, lived with their paternal uncle, Furman Seawright, and his family in Sawyerdale, located in western Orangeburg County. They lived on the property owned by John H. Corbett, Sr., who was one of Sawyerdale's leading citizens and respectable farmers.[59][60][61][62] Among the children in the household, Robert was the oldest and worked as a farm laborer alongside his uncle and brother. The family were members of Antioch Missionary Baptist Church, which was near where they lived.[63]

On February 22, 1921, Furman's wife, Ella, died at the age of thirty-three.[64][65] Ella's death significantly impacted Furman, Robert, and the entire family. A few years later, Furman was remarried to Mary **Piper**, who had children from a previous marriage.[66] Searching for better opportunities, they relocated to Cleveland, Ohio. In Cleveland, Furman worked at a steel mill.[67][68]

---

53   Ancestry.com. 1910 United States Federal Census.

54   Arthur Seawright is buried at Smyrna Missionary Baptist Church, Springfield, South Carolina.

55   Annie Mae Johnson Seawright is buried at Smyrna Missionary Baptist Church, Springfield, South Carolina.

56   Robert's sister Mattie lived with their paternal grandparents Joseph and Martha Kitchings Seawright Ellison. Robert's other sisters lived with their maternal grandmother, Alfer Williams Johnson, and their uncle, Boatis Johnson.

57   FamilySearch.org. 1920 United States Federal Census.

58   Ancestry.com. 1920 United States Federal Census.

59   Furman's wife name was Ella Davis Seawright. Their children were: Martha Seawright, Olivia Seawright, Dorothy Seawright, Johnnie (Jimbuck) Seawright, Beatrice Seawright, and Clara Seawright.

60   Ancestry.com. 1920 United States Federal Census.

61   Ancestry.com. U.S., World War I Draft Registration Cards, 1917–1918.

62   The property was located on present day Hwy 394 (Salley Road) adjacent to Woodbine Road in Sawyerdale in western Orangeburg County.

63   Antioch Missionary Baptist Church is located near Sawyerdale.

64   Ancestry.com. South Carolina Death Records, 18211968.

65   Ella is buried at Antioch Missionary Baptist Church, Sawyerdale Community, South Carolina.

66   Ancestry.com. 1930 United States Federal Census.

67   Furman and Mary Seawright and their family lived on 2540 E 40th Street, Cleveland, Ohio.

68   Ancestry.com. U.S. City Directories, 1822–1995.

He left his children from Ella in the care of other relatives. [69] [70] On March 7th, 1936, Furman died at the age of 49.[71] [72] [73] [74]

Shortly after Furman's departure, in 1925, Robert married Alice Thompson, the daughter of Oscar J. and Frances Coats Thompson.[75] Alice was very reserved, humble, an excellent cook, and like Robert, a farm laborer.[76] They were blessed with six children; however, only four were born: Arthur Seawright, Wallace Seawright, Sr., Wilson Seawright, and Catherine Seawright McCollough.[77] [78] [79] [80] The family settled in the Hollow Creek Community, near Perry, South Carolina; then, in the mid-1930s, they moved to the New Holland Community north of Wagener, South Carolina.[81] [82] [83] While living on the farm, Robert would allow his neighbors to draw well water which was near his house.[84] Like his father, Robert was a tenant farmer who embraced an entrepreneurial spirit and earned income selling goat meat and in skilled trade jobs.

Like many human personalities, there are upsides and shortcomings. Robert's upsides were his charisma and sense of humor. One day, a cousin saw him working in the fields. Robert replied, "I am packing sand for the good ole USA."[85] His daughter, Catherine, saw him walking the streets

---

69   Ancestry.com. 1930 United States Federal Census.

70   Furman brother, Kirkland Seawright, and his wife Annie Schofield raised Furman daughters, Beatrice and Clara.

71   FamilySearch.org, Ohio Deaths, 1908–1953.

72   During the time of Furman's death, he lived on 2201 E 90 Street, Cleveland, Ohio.

73   Find A Grave. http://www.findagrave.com/cgi-bin/fg.cgi.

74   Furman Seawright is buried at Harvard Grove Cemetery, Cleveland. Ohio.

75   Ancestry.com. 1930 United States Federal Census.

76   Alice was known for baking desserts, especially apple pies, peach pies, and pound cake.

77   Arthur Seawright was named after Robert's father and son. Robert's son, Arthur died in a car accident due to Robert's intoxication from alcohol. The accident took place at night, after the family left church service.

78   In-person conversation with Otis Corbitt., son of John and Thelma Ellison Corbitt.

79   Wallace Seawright, Sr. was named after Alice's maternal uncle, Wallace Coats.

80   Wilson Seawright was name after Robert's first cousin, Wilson Seawright.

81   Ancestry.com. 1930 United States Federal Census.

82   Alice half siblings, Lumanda Thompson Williams and Purvis "Bush" Thompson, Jr., shared in babysitting duties watching over Wallace, Wilson, and Catherine.

83   Ancestry.com. 1940 United States Federal Census.

84   In-person conversation with Leroy Gantt, husband of Barbra Jean Wooden Gantt.

85   In-person conversation with Essie Pontoo, daughter of Ocie and Essie L. Johnson.

and told her, "Baby I work on Park Street. I parked the car and walk the streets all day." [86] [87] Robert also had the gift of gab with a grin. One day, he persuaded his first cousin, Thelma Corbitt, to eat his goat meat. He said to her, "Cuz I prepared this goat meat for you, I want you to try some." [88] In contrast, Robert's shortcomings were his sternness and stinginess. Sometimes when he was intoxicated, Robert chastised his wife and told his son, Wallace, that he would be punished for not fighting his classmate who harassed him. [89] [90] One day, during a large gathering at Smyrna Missionary Baptist Church, several men gave Robert money to purchase liquor. [91] Robert bought the liquor but refused to share it. This incident invoked the ire of Sam Brown who wanted to fight him. Luckily for Robert, his brother-in-law, Andrew Rowe, protected him and fought Sam. Robert watched and said, "There go old Andrew Rowe fighting now." A heated incident occurred when Robert's sister-in-law, Dorothy Thompson Jones, was gossiping. [92] Robert was so upset that he threatened to harm her, but his son, Wilson, intervened.

On December 7, 1941, Japanese aircraft attacked the major US naval base at Pearl Harbor in Hawaii, taking the Americans by surprise and claiming the lives of more than 2,300 troops. The attack on Pearl Harbor resulted in Congress declaring war on Japan on December 8, 1941 and the United States entering World War II. The war effort required production of necessities such as clothing for troops; led to an industrialization boom across the country that created jobs. Southern urban cities, such as Columbia, South Carolina, had mills that produced cloth that prospered during the war and employed thousands of people. In early 1942, Robert moved to Columbia and was employed at Pacific Mills as a laborer. [93] [94] [95] Pacific Mills produced 350 million yards of fabric for the war effort, which made uniforms, shirts, shorts, sheets, mattress covers, raincoats, and camouflage items. While living in Columbia, Robert stayed with his brother Gadsden, who lived in the historic Ward One community, which was home to many African Americans as early

---

86   In-person conversation with Catherine Seawright McCollough, daughter of Robert L. and Alice Thompson.

87   Park Street located in the historic Ward 1 Community in Columbia, South Carolina. Robert frequently hung out on this street during the time he stayed there.

88   In-person conversation with Otis Corbitt, son of John and Thelma Ellison Corbitt.

89   In-person conversation with Michael Seawright, son of Wilson and Nancy Johnson Seawright.

90   In-person conversation with Arthur Seawright, son of Wallace and Armenia Wooden Seawright.

91   In-person conversation with Rev. Mack Staley, son of Paul and Ella Holmes Staley.

92   In-person conversation with Nancy Johnson Seawright, wife of Wilson Seawright.

93   Ancestry.com. U.S. WWII Draft Cards Young Men, 1940–1947.

94   In 1942, Robert L. Seawright with his brother, Gadsden, on 522 Sumter Street, Columbia, South Carolina.

95   Pacific Millis is known as Olympia Mills.

as the Reconstruction era.[96] The community attracted many rural residents like Robert who were looking for urban work to escape farming life and plentiful recreational amenities. The community had its own cultural identity reflected in entrepreneurship, educational institutions, and bustling churches.

The era known as the Great Migration was the widespread migration of African Americans in the 20th century from rural communities in the South to the urban cities in the North and West. Historians have estimated that there were over 6 million African Americans who migrated relocated. Facing the harshness of Jim Crow Laws, limited economic opportunities, and poor wages, southern African Americans migrated for prospective hope of a better quality of life. Recognizing the opportunity, in 1957, Robert and Alice moved to New York City and resided in the city's borough of Queens.[97] [98] With the help of her half-sister, Alice was employed as a housekeeper in Jewish households throughout the city boroughs, and Robert was employed as a construction laborer and earned extra money by collecting bottles and cans.[99] [100] [101] Later, their children, Wilson and Catherine, along with their families, moved to New York City. Occasionally, Robert and Alice would return to Salley during the summer months to visit their son, Wallace and his growing family.[102] Robert and Alice would bring clothes for the family. They enjoyed spending time with their grandchildren.

In 1960, Robert was experiencing health problems from the northern climate in New York City. His doctor told him to relocate back home to Salley because of favorable climate conditions.[103] In the summer of 1960, Robert's health was declining. A near-death incident occurred when Robert passed out during a shopping trip in Aiken, only to be revived by an indoor desk fan.[104] On the morning of July 7, 1960, Robert's granddaughter, Cheryl, was instructed by her

---

96   Bouknight, A. N. (2010). "Casualty of Progress": The Ward One Community and Urban Renewal, Columbia, South Carolina, 1964-1974; retrieved from https://scholarcommons.sc.edu/etd/142.

97   Before moving to New York City, Alice sold fifty acres of land given to her by her aunt, Carrie Coats Friday, as an inheritance for $238.21. She sold it to Ted T. Busbee. The land was located on State Highway, five miles west of the town of Salley, South Carolina.

98   Deed from Alice Seawright to Ted T. Busbee, 7 November 1957 (filed 8 November 1957), Aiken County, South Carolina, Title Book No.207, p.270, Clerk of Court for Aiken County.

99   In-person conversation with Romeo Ellison, son of Jerome and Dollie Ellison.

100   Ancestry.com. South Carolina, Death Records, 1821–1968.

101   In-person conversation with Romeo Ellison, son of Jerome and Dollie Ellison.

102   In-person conversation with Cheryl Seawright Curry, daughter of Wallace and Armenia Wooden Seawright.

103   In-person conversation with Arthur Seawright, son of Wallace and Armenia Wooden Seawright.

104   In-person conversation with Arthur Seawright.

mother to wake Robert up for breakfast. He did not and died suddenly from pneumonia.[105] [106] On July 28, 1960, Robert was funeralized.[107]

After Robert's death, Alice returned to New York City, working and living with her children , and briefly with her half-sister, Lumanda Thompson Williams, and her family.[108] [109] In 1966, Alice relocated back to Salley **and lived** next door to her son, Wallace, and his family.[110] Alice spent considerable time with her grandchildren, siblings, nieces, and nephews, and she even had a companion named Charlie Rowe.[111] [112] [113] On January 12, 1969, Alice died at the age of the age of sixty-three.
[114]

Despite his shortcomings, Robert used joviality and grittiness to navigate his life. As the only son of his parents to become a progenitor, Robert's resolve made it possible for the Seawright bloodline to continue: three children, twenty-eight grandchildren, and over 100 great-grandchildren, and counting.

During life challenges, Robert confronted them through humor. Despite the fact his parents died young before the age of ten, Robert demonstrated resolve that made it possible for him to raise a family, to work, and to live.

---

105   In-person conversation with Cheryl Seawright Curry, daughter of Wallace and Armenia Wooden Seawright.

106   Ancestry.com. South Carolina, Death Records, 1821–1968.

107   Ancestry.com. South Carolina, Death Records, 1821–1968.

108   Alice lived with her son, Wilson, and his family, at 152–27 118th Avenue, Jamaica, Queens, New York.

109   Alice helped raised Lumanda children. During the holidays, she would cook a big feast for the family.

110   Alice lived on 320 Hunter Branch Road, Salley, South Carolina.

111   Alice grandson, Roosevelt Seawright, son of Wilson and Nancy Mae Johnson Seawright, said that Alice made thick, large biscuits. Alice was known for her cooking. Her favorite recipes were baked ham, brownies, and homemade cakes.

112   Alice's nephew, Roosevelt "Hump" Rowe, son of Andrew and Gladys Thompson Rowe, said that Alice was like a second mother to him and provided counsel when needed.

113   Charlie Rowe was the father of Alice brother-in-law, Andrew Rowe.

114   Robert and Alice are buried at Smyrna Missionary Baptist Church, Springfield, South Carolina.

Defined by Moral Values and Clever Foresight of Wisdom: The Story of Wallace Seawright, Sr.

"Traditional, historical American values have in the past, included a faith in God, prayer and the Bible, which has for a large part, been the foundation of other national traditions. These included such things as honor and respect for the family, diligent work ethics, absolute values of right and wrong, and taking responsibility to provide for our own—such as one's spouse, family and children, and so forth"—Dale A. Robbins

"Don't anybody determine how you are. That is your job and responsibility"—Wallace Seawright, Sr.

Wallace Seawright, Sr., the oldest child of Robert Lee and Alice Thompson Seawright, was born on March 3, 1927, in Hollow Creek Community, near Perry, South Carolina.[115] At an early age, Wallace attended Gum Ridge School near Wagener, South Carolina. In school, he excelled in his studies especially in literacy.[116] After the eighth grade, Wallace quit school to help his family although his education was not limited.[117] Under his father's tutelage, Wallace learned valuable knowledge and skills in trades, agriculture, frugality, and entrepreneurship. Growing up in his parents' household as the oldest child, Wallace had responsibilities placed upon him. He protected his siblings, Wilson and Catherine. Wallace was given household authority when his father left home to work or left home unexpectedly without anybody knowing where he was.

---

115 Ancestry.com. 1930 United States Federal Census.

116 In-person conversation with Catherine Seawright McCollough, daughter of Robert and Alice Thompson Seawright.

117 In-person conversation with Cheryl Seawright Curry, daughter of Wallace and Armenia Wooden Seawright.

In the early 1930s, Wallace and his family moved from Hollow Creek to the New Holland community north of Wagener.[118] In 1936, at the age of nine, Wallace joined Baughmanville Baptist Church, located in the same vicinity where he lived.[119] As a member, Wallace was ordained as a deacon, joined the Senior Choir, and mentored both children and adults. To further his spiritual growth, Wallace joined Prince Hall Masonic Order as a member of Jerusalem Lodge #400. He actively participated in lodge activities and formulated lifelong relationships with his fellow brethren.

Once upon a time, churches were places where men and women courted each other. Friendship Baptist Church was where Wallace met his wife, Armenia Wooden, the youngest daughter of Harry J. and Annie Reed Wooden Bolton.[120] Wallace and Armenia were married in 1946.[121] Their union was blessed with twenty-two children; sixteen children were born: Wallace Seawright, Jr., Barbra Seawright Garvin, Arthur L. Seawright, Robert L. Seawright, Cheryl Seawright Curry, Catherine Seawright Garvin, Corine Seawright Leaphart, Willie Seawright, Ronnie Seawright, Armenia Seawright Wright, Alice Seawright, Annette Seawright Patterson, Roosevelt Seawright, Artis Seawright, Dorothy Seawright Landy, and Gregory L. Seawright. The family lived on several farms in the Wagener and Salley area, which included New Holland and Rustin communities.

Individually, Wallace was very principled and acted in accordance with morality and recognized what was right and wrong. He strongly believed in the institution of marriage; refused to accept government assistance to provide clothing and free school lunch for his children until later; and abhorred gossip and lying and helping others. Wallace strongly practiced frugality and was thrifty with money and food. Some folks in the community would marvel about Wallace's frugal habits and believed he was rich. Moreover, Wallace assisted his relatives and friends in times of need. Wallace provided food and clothing to his sister-in-law, Nancy Seawright, and her children. Wallace briefly raised his nephew, Jackson McCollough. During recreation times, Wallace enjoyed hunting wild game and participating in church-related activities.[122] [123]

As the head of the household, Wallace was a devoted husband, father, and convivial. As a husband, he was devoted to his wife Armenia, and they were devoted to each other. Personality wise, they were opposites. Wallace was quite talkative but reserved at times. Armenia was very talkative

---

118   Ancestry.com. United States Word War II Draft Cards Young Men, 1940–1947.

119   In-person conversation with Catherine S. McCollough.

120   Interview with Robert L. Seawright, son of Wallace and Armenia Wooden Seawright.

121   Wallace was eighteen years old, and Armenia was fourteen years old when they got married.

122   Wallace hunted rabbits and squirrels.

123   Wallace had a shotgun named Betsy. Every New Year's Day at 12:00 a.m., he would fire the shot in the air to

too but boastful and jovial. She was known as a "straight shooter" who spoke how she felt. In a conversation, Armenia jokingly said to Wallace, "When I first met you, I loved you so much that I could have ate you, now that I am married to you, I wish I hadn't ate you."[124] As a father, Wallace required his children to attend school and church and complete daily chores. He did not allow fighting or encourage it, except for one incident when he told his sons to wrangle each other in a circle he drew on the ground.[125] [126] Children were given chores to complete. The eldest children were given supervisory responsibilities over the younger children. Despite his strictness, Wallace showed benevolence toward his children by demonstrating charity and imparted wisdom. Convivially, family traditions of celebrating holidays, birthdays, and social gatherings were commonplace. During Christmas time, Wallace brought his children gifts. Birthday parties and social gatherings were very frequent. Relatives and friends alike would come to fellowship with Wallace and his family.

During his early years of employment, Wallace was a very active sharecropper who grew cotton, fruits, and vegetables but yielded little income. Like many other sharecroppers, Wallace and his family had to work extremely hard to provide one half or third of the crop to their landowner to pay rent. Wallace children did not attend school until all the cotton was picked during harvest time, which was usually in October. Wallace children were occasionally teased by other children when the school bus drove by the fields where they worked.[127] Because sharecropping yielded little income and kept his family in debt, Wallace contemplated moving his family to Washington, D.C., where his wife's siblings lived, but decided to stay and continue sharecropping.[128] In the early 1960s, Wallace supplemented his sharecropping income as a construction laborer for Daniel Construction, a company that built residential barracks at Fort Jackson. [129 130 131]

---

124   Interview with Robert L. Seawright.

125   Ibid

126   The sons were Willie and Ronnie Seawright. Their wrangle ended in a draw. After that, Wallace rebuked them both.

127   In-person conversation with Cheryl Seawright Curry, daughter of Wallace and Armenia Wooden Seawright.

128   In-person conversation with Arthur L. Seawright, son of Wallace and Armenia Wooden Seawright.

Occasionally, **Wallace** would hired out his oldest sons and other sharecroppers to work for other landowners for additional income.[132] [133] [134]

On June 2, 1964, President Lydon B. Johnson signed the Civil Rights Act of 1964, which outlawed discrimination based on race, color, religion, sex, national origin, sexual orientation, and prohibited employment discrimination. A few years after the law was enacted, the South's largest industry, textile manufacturing, underwent radical changes in the racial composition of its workforce. Previously, African Americans were barred from textile mill jobs; but that ended under the act. In South Carolina, less than five percent of mill employees were African American in 1964.[135] Between 1960 and 1969, African Americans employment in textile mills increased four times faster than the national average for all manufacturing.[136] In 1969, Wallace was employed as a draw frame operator at the Hickman Mill of the Graniteville Manufacturing Company, a major textile manufacturing company located in Graniteville, South Carolina, until his retirement in 1982.[137] Draw frame operators operated the draw frame machine, ensured proper feeding of carded or combed sliver, pieced the sliver on breakage, doffed the sliver cans, and transported the delivery cans to the storage area. This job required the individual to have thorough knowledge of process flow and material flow in a textile mill for yarn production, and they had to know the important functions and operations of all the machines in drawing department. During Wallace's tenure at Graniteville, international demand for denim cotton fabric and increased demand from clothing stores to fill their inventories during the recession contributed to the company's success.[138] In 1976, the Hickman Mill instituted a 10 million expansion program that added 100 jobs to the company, 6,000 positions at that time.[139] Being employed at Graniteville Manufacturing Company was a saving grace for Wallace, due to the decline of sharecropping that began in the late 1960s and

---

129   Interview with Robert L. Seawright, son of Wallace and Armenia Wooden Seawright.

130   Fort Jackson is located near Columbia, South Carolina.

131   Telephone conservation with Arthur L. Seawright, son of Wallace and Armenia Wooden Seawright.

132   In-person conversation with Robert L. Seawright.

133   The landowners were Wallace's uncle, Purvis "Bush" Thompson, Jr., and his father-in-law, Johnnie Williams.

134   Wallace was a farm manager of several farms owned by the Brodie family.

135   Minchin, Timothy J. Black Activism, the 1964 Civil Rights Act, and the Radical Integration of the Southern Textile Industry" The Journal of Southern History 65, no.4 (1999): 809–44.

136   Minchin, Timothy J. Black Activism.

137   "Retirements," Graniteville Bulletin, n.d.

138   "Aiken County Economy." The Aiken Standard, September 30, 1975; retrieved from www.newspapers.com.

139   "Aiken County Economy."

early 1970s; and due to mechanization of farm work that resulted in sharecroppers being forced to relocate from the farms to urban cities for employment.

In 1970, Wallace purchased a three-bedroom brick house on Hunter Branch Road in the Rustin Community.[140] The family lived in the house for three years until 1973 when due to falling behind on mortgage payments, the house was sold. The family relocated to a permanent house on Inkberry Road, which was a few miles away. Furthermore, Wallace became a young grandfather at the age of forty-three with the birth of his oldest grandchild and grandson, Terry Jackson.[141] [142] After Terry, more grandchildren were born during his lifetime and they included the following: Anthony Seawright, Keith Seawright, Lamont Seawright, Patricia Garvin, Michael Garvin, Gregory Garvin, Cheryl Garvin, Robert Corley, III, Cynthia Garvin, Willie Seawright, Jr., Brandon Seawright, Amanda Seawright, Kelvin Seawright, Walter B. Curry, Jr., Felicia Seawright, Latasha Daniels, Tyrone Garvin, Omelia Nicole Seawright, Marcus Corley, Jason Seawright, Kendall Seawright, Eric Garvin, and Lakeshia Seawright.

The year 1984 was a tragic year for Wallace and the family. On December 3, 1984, at the age of fifty-three, Wallace's wife, Armenia, died, due to heart issues. After the death of his wife a few months later, Wallace became very ill and relocated to a nursing home in Augusta, Georgia. On September 3, 1985, at the age of fifty-eight, Wallace died.[143]

Roy E. Disney, the nephew of the legendary Walt Disney, quoted, "When your values are clear to you, making decisions become easier." Value is defined as something of importance that influences decisions on what actions are best to do or to live. As a deacon, Wallace valued the Christian faith by serving his church. As a husband, father, and grandfather, Wallace valued the dignity of his wife, children, and grandchildren and created a culture of love rooted in discipline, wisdom, and compassion. As a man of labor, Wallace used his clever foresight to escape the trappings of sharecropping by supplementing his income doing formal work with benefits and guaranteed income. As a member of the community, Wallace valued his friends and relatives. Despite their circumstances and personalities, **Wallace** saw the good in them.

According to the great philosopher Plato, some men value honor, some men value profit, but the "philosopher king" values wisdom, intelligence, reliability, and a willingness to live a simple life. Wallace was a philosopher king in his own right, in his own way.

---

140   Interview with Robert L. Seawright, son of Wallace and Armenia Wooden Seawright.

141   Terry Jackson father is Arthur L. Seawright, son of Wallace and Armenia Wooden Seawright.

142   Terry Jackson was born in 1970.

143   Wallace and Armenia are buried at Baughmanville Baptist Church, Wagener, South Carolina.

Men of Value: The Stories of Roosevelt & Henry Edward Seawright

"Try not to become a man of success, but rather try to become a man of value."
—*Albert Einstein*

"The community may not at that time be prepared for, or feel the need of, Greek analysis, but it may feel it needs of bricks and house and wagons. If the man can supply the need for those, then, it will lead eventually to a demand for the first product, and with the demand will come the ability to appreciate it and to profit it by."—*Booker T. Washington*

Roosevelt Seawright, the oldest son of Wilson and Eliza Edwards Seawright, was born on June 5, 1933 near Springfield, South Carolina.[144] [145] [146] At an early age, he attended Aiken County public schools and joined Oakey Springs Missionary Baptist Church near Salley, South Carolina.

In the late 1940s, Roosevelt's parents moved to Aiken, South Carolina. At the time, Aiken had a thriving African American community. There were many successful African American owned businesses, and many people had several jobs to provide a better quality of life for their families. African Americans who lived in rural Aiken County moved to Aiken for better employment opportunities, educational advancement, suitable housing, a robust recreational, and social life.

---

144   Wilson and Eliza Edwards daughters were Mildred S. Patterson and Martha s. Minor. He also had a son, Hazel Seawright, from his first cousin, Beatrice Seawright.

145   Wilson was self-employed early in his working life, a sharecropper, and a truck driver who hauled livestock while living in Aiken, South Carolina.

146   Eliza was a homemaker.

In 1952, Roosevelt married Louise Jenkins at the local courthouse.[147] Their union were bless-ed with four children: Patricia Seawright Adams, Sharon Seawright Childs, Reginald "Reggie" Seawright, Ronald "Ronnie" Seawright, and Renee Seawright. The family attended Welcome Traveler Baptist Church where Roosevelt joined under Christian experience and sang on the Gospel Choir.

In 1957, Roosevelt pursued the tradesmen craft of brick masonry as a helper. Then in 1960, Roosevelt became a brick mason.[148] As a brick mason, Roosevelt was a very skilled and experienced tradesperson who laid bricks and blocks without supervision and provided supervision to less-skilled workers. Roosevelt was employed with Gents and Associates, Schaeffer Builders, and Bill Gainer Builders. Roosevelt did brick work throughout the Aiken area, Beech Island, Jackson, and North Augusta, South Carolina. Roosevelt bricked his own home and homes in several prominent communities, which included Governs Acres and Gatewood Subdivision.[149] Roosevelt, along with his brother Henry, helped with the building of Montmorenci Missionary Baptist Church and Smith Hazel Recreational Center in Aiken, named after Josie Hazel and Jason Smith who were community activists who gave money to build it.[150]

Roosevelt was very ambitious, stern, and self-conscious. Roosevelt was very conscious of his appear-ance and dress apart. Roosevelt loved food and was very particular about his food. Roosevelt believed a home should be cleaned, with everyone doing their part, and he would "suffer no fools" when it came to himself and his family.[151] Furthermore, as a husband and father, Roosevelt took his roles very seriously with pride. Roosevelt was a provider who worked hard and ardently believed in self-reliance in taking care of his family.[152] Roosevelt made sure that his family had the necessities of living and instilled a work ethic among his children and grandchildren. Roosevelt mentored his sons in brick masonry and bricked homes for his daughters.[153]

147   Louise met Roosevelt at St. Noah Church on Charleston Street (at that time was called Winfield Town) in Aiken, SC.

148   Roosevelt worked at the Savannah River Site in the 1950s.

149   Roosevelt built houses on Pine Long Road and South Boundary & Hwy 1 in Aiken, South Carolina.

150   The Center of African American History, Art, and Culture (2008). A Pictorial History of African Americans in Aiken County, edited by T. Ella Strother.

151   Roosevelt did not tolerate ignorant people or behavior. An individual had to stay in his place around his family, and he did not hesitate to confront people talking negatively about his family.

152   Roosevelt allowed his daughter, Sharon, to take the family car to college.

As a grandfather, Roosevelt was more like a father to his oldest grandsons, Marcus and Brian, and made sure that the grandchildren would eat whenever they came over to visit.

The relationship Roosevelt had with his siblings were good. He and his brother, Henry, were inseparable. They had that brotherly bond. Roosevelt had a good relationship with his sisters, Mildred and Martha Ann, also. He was admired by many of his nieces, nephews, cousins, and other relatives.

Roosevelt was liked in the community by many people who looked up to him. He tried to mentor the young men in his presence to work for a living. They would come to Roosevelt for advice and address him as "Mr. Sea." Many young men would come around when Roosevelt barbecued hogs during the holidays. They would sit with him all night while Roosevelt grilled the hog.

Roosevelt's brother, Henry Edward Seawright, the youngest son of Wilson and Eliza Edward Seawright, was born on November 21, 1941, near Salley, South Carolina. At an early age, Henry joined Oakey Springs Missionary Baptist Church near Salley, South Carolina. When Henry family moved to Aiken in the late 1940s, Henry attended Martha Schofield High School.[154] After high school, Henry relocated to Hempstead, New York, where he worked as a chef in Stevenson's Restaurant at the racetrack.

Upon returning to South Carolina, Henry married Shirley Mae McKevie.[155] Their union was blessed with three daughters: Connie Seawright, Michelle Seawright, and Stephanie Seawright Smith. As the head of the household, Henry was a very devoted husband and father. He taught his children self-independence and was very strict.[156] Henry was very fond of his grandchildren: all grandsons.[157] During the event of his wife's illness and passing, Henry reinvigorated his faith and joined Ashely Grove Missionary Baptist Church in Aiken, where he served faithfully.[158] Vocationally, Henry was a stellar contractor in skilled trades. Henry's love and passion for carpentry took him to another level; for Henry could create and build something for nothing.

---

153   Roosevelt built his oldest daughter's, Patricia's, house in 1978, which she currently lives in. He worked for Schaeffer Builders during that time. Roosevelt bricked his youngest daughter's, Renee's, house in 1991, located on Pine Log Road in Aiken, South Carolina.

154   Henry was an avid pool player and played pool at Davis Place in Aiken, South Carolina.

155   Henry was a very sharp dresser and wore Kango hats.

156   Henry built wheelbarrows for his daughters and gave them shovels to do yard work. He taught them to paint and cut their wood.

157   Henry would pick up his grandson "KT" from the bus stop during school week. Henry's grandson Lamario kept a dog at his house.

158   Henry had a special seat where he sat at church.

Henry built wheelbarrows, security bars, chifforobes, keepsake boxes, bedstep stools, and storage benches with cushions.[159] Henry was also a brick mason. Henry and his brother Roosevelt collaborated on several projects, which included Smith-Hazel Recreation Center and Montmorenci Missionary Baptist Church in Aiken.[160]

On March 5, 1998, Roosevelt died at Aiken Regional Medical Center.[161] Sixteen years later, on July 14, 2014, Henry died.[162] Roosevelt & Henry work in brick masonry is legendary in the Aiken community. Local citizens still marvel about their quality of excellence and craftmanship that is unrivaled. Roosevelt & Henry valued the sense of meaning, purpose, and contribution to their families and communities.

---

159   Henry built and made things for his daughters, which included security bars, chifforobes, keep sake boxes, bed step stools, and storage benches.

160   Henry helped Roosevelt build his Patricia's and Renee's homes.

161   Roosevelt is buried at Sunset Memorial Gardens, Graniteville, South Carolina.

162   Henry is buried at Ashley Grove Missionary Baptist Church, Aiken, South Carolina.

Generational Pillars of their Community: The Story of Floster "Tan" and Nora Miles Ellison, Sr.

"Carve your name on hearts, not tombstones. A legacy is etched into the minds of others and the stories they share about you."-Shannon Adler

Floster "Tan" Ellison, Sr., the oldest son of Joseph and Martha Kitchings Seawright Ellison, was born on October 1, 1886 near Salley, South Carolina. During his childhood, Floster spent most of this time on the farm. He learned the value of independence and industry under the tutelage of his father, who was a pine tree surveyor and landowner. Floster was loved and respected by his family and was a leader among his siblings.

In 1908, Floster married Nora Miles, the daughter of Lewis and Victoria Pope Miles. Their union was blessed with ten children: Thelma Ellison Corbitt, Victoria Ellison, Joe Louis Ellison, Ausbon Ellison, Holly Ellison, Floster L Ellison, Jr., James Ellison, Nannie Ellison Ware, Geneva Ellison Brown, Allie Mae Zeigler Wilson, Mary Ellison, and Martha Ellison Oliver. The family lived on rented property in the Hollow Creek Community near Perry, South Carolina, then later moved to the Sawyerdale community in western Orangeburg County.[163] While living in Sawyerdale, the family attended Antioch Missionary Baptist Church which was nearby.[164]

Floster and Nora were tenant farmers. Being tenant farmers, they had their own tools and animals and a rent for the land and housing stipulated by the landowner. Compared to sharecroppers,

---

163   Telephone conversation with Martha E. Oliver, daughter of Floster T. and Nora Ellison Miles.

164   According to Floster L. Ellison, Jr. took almost a day in the wagon from Sawyerdale to Smyrna Missionary Baptist Church because the mules had to be fed and watered along the way. Since they lived in Sawyerdale and Antioch Missionary Baptist Church was nearby, a decision was made to attend Antioch.

tenant farmers had more freedom and flexibility, but both tenant farmers and sharecroppers' earnings were very low. The gross average income for tenant famers was under $400. [165]

The plight of tenant farming encouraged some farmers and their families to diversify their income. Floster diversified his income as an entrepreneur. He owned and operated a sugar cane mill. The sugar cane mill was powered by a mule that walked around a circle that guided the long sticks to generate power that crushed the sugar cane stalks. The cane juice was extracted, transferred into a kettle for cooking that produced sorghum syrup sold to customers.[166] Floster also owned and operated a millet grinder that he used to grind millet seeds for customers.[167] In addition to being an entrepreneur, Floster frequently relocated to Detroit, Michigan to work to make additional money for his family.[168] Because of his work ethic, Floster enjoyed the fruits of his labor and purchased a Model T Ford family car.[169]

Floster was very literate and believed in education. He led the effort to build a school, St. Paul Elementary, for African American children in Saywerdale.[170] St. Paul served students in grades one through eight.[171] The school only had one teacher, who taught reading, math, science, and social studies. The older students helped with the smaller students. The physical structure of the school was a little barn with one window and shelves for the books. During the winter months, students brought coal and sticks to make the fire. Students stayed in school for seven to nine months and brought their lunches.

Nora was a professional caregiver who cared for the sick and those in need from all backgrounds.[172] She made home visits on occasions for pneumonia-stricken people and other health conditions. As a Cherokee Indian, Nora was knowledgeable in holistic herb medicine and partnered with Charlie Lyles Company. She also assisted Dr. Johnny Brodie, who owned a physician practice in Wagener, South Carolina. Nora is a member of a legacy of African American women

---

165   "Tenant Farming in the South." The Times and Democrat, March 06, 1937; retrieved from www.newspapers.com.

166   Martha E. Oliver. "Family History." New York, n.d.

167   Millet seeds were used to make flour or alcoholic drinks.

168   Telephone conversation with Martha E. Oliver, daughter of Floster and Nora Miles Ellison.

169   Telephone conversation with Martha E. Oliver.

170   Ibid.

171   In-person conversation with Flora Dunbar Harris, former student of Saint Paul Elementary School located in Sawyerdale.

172   Martha E. Oliver.

caregivers in the Wagener-Salley area that included Geneva Benjamin, Josephine Matthews, Clyde Stroman, and others.

In the 1940s, the Ellison family purchased 500 acres of land west of Salley, South Carolina and settled into a new life of independence and opportunities.[173] They reinstated their membership at Smyrna Missionary Baptist Church, where Floster was ordained as a deacon and served briefly as church treasurer. Nora also served faithfully as a deaconess and helped orchestrated baptism services and prepared grape wine for Holy Communion services.[174] The 1940s were also a tragic time for the family. In 1944, Nora's brother, Pickens Miles, died at the age of forty-six, followed by his wife, Lucille, who died in 1945, at the age of thirty-seven. Because of the close relationship Nora had with her brother and his wife, she along with Floster, raised their children, Arthur Lee Miles, Nora Miles, Mildred Miles, Pickens Carnel Miles, Wendell Miles, and Geraldine Miles, as their own.[175] In 1946, Floster and Nora's oldest son, Ausbon Ellison, died at the age of thirty-three.

Despite these challenges, Floster and Nora continued to preserve. In 1950, Floster, along with several African American farmers in Aiken County, engaged in soil-conservation practices on their land.[176] In addition, Floster and Nora witnessed their children and grandchildren matriculate into adulthood. Some of them were educators, college students, college graduates, businessmen, acclaimed musicians, community leaders, virtuous and charismatic individuals in the community.

On October 29, 1959, Nora died at the age of seventy-two.[177] Six years later, in 1965, Floster died at the age of seventy-nine. Their lives can be defined as being exemplars of service in their respective occupations, family, and community. They created a culture of love within their family and community. They were indeed generational pillars of their community.

---

173   Ibid

174   Martha E. Oliver. "Family History." New York, n.d.

175   Telephone conversation with Martha E. Oliver, daughter of Floster and Nora Miles Ellison.

176   "Negro Farmers Increase Soil Conservation." The Aiken Standard, July 28, 1950; retrieved from www.newspapers.com.

177   Ancestry.com. South Carolina, U.S., Death Records, 1821-1968.

The Legendary "Mr. Superstar of Gospel"—The Story of Tommy Ellison

"Inspired by Leaving a Legacy"—Stephanie Lehart

"Many songs from different music genres come and go, but gospel music lives forever. You can play any gospel song at any given time and still have the same feeling when you first heard it"-Tommy Ellison

Tommy Ellison, son of Ausbon and Ida Mae McKie Ellison Parker, was born on September 15, 1932, near Salley, South Carolina.[178] When he was a toddler, Tommy parents moved to New York City and settled in Harlem during the height of the Harlem Renaissance, a blossoming era of African American culture in the creative arts and literature. Harlem was the symbolic capital of the cultural awakening of African Americans across the country. Harlem gave creative space through the arts and literature to address African American culture, civil rights, and social justice issues. Many famous African American intellectuals and artists lived during the Harlem Renaissance. While living in Harlem, Ausbon was employed at the famous Hotel Theresa, a thirteen-story hotel with 300 guest rooms. It was the largest hotel in Harlem and one of the few hotels in New York City that welcomed African American guests. Hotel Theresa hosted many prominent American figures, foreign dignitaries, and was a meeting place that birthed racial and social justice movements.[179]

At the age of four, Tommy moved in with his grandparents, Floster "Tan" and Nora Miles Ellison. Along with his fathers' siblings, Floster and Nora raised Tommy as their own son. Tommy

---

178   Ausbon Ellison died in 1945 and is buried at Smyrna Missionary Baptist Church, Springfield, South Carolina.

179   Wilson, Sondra Kathryn. "Meet Me at the Theresa: The Story of Harlem's Most Famous Hotel," 2004. p.205.

was their oldest grandchild.[180] At an early age, **Tommy** attended Piney Grove School and joined Smyrna Missionary Baptist Church, where he sang on the children's choir.[181] While going to school and working in the fields, Tommy would boast to his friends and relatives that someday he would be famous.

Encouraged by his grandmother, who advised him to "sing for the Lord," Tommy embraced traditional African American gospel.[182] This form of music expresses personal and communal beliefs regarding African American Christian life. The music originated from the cultural experiences of enslaved West Africans integrated with Western Christianity that emerged into spirituals. Enslaved Africans used spirituals to pass on hidden messages to escape, share life experiences and joyous times. After emancipation and into the early 20th century, the spirituals matriculated into African American churches, which simultaneously embraced Protestant gospel songs. In addition, some African American gospel musicians like Thomas Dorsey during the early 20th century, began to infuse the blues, a music genre originated in the South by African Americans distinguished by a strong rhythm, shouts, chants, and lyrical repetition.[183] Dorsey, a Georgia native known as the father of gospel music, was influential in the development of early blues and 20th century gospel music with songs such as "Take My Hand, Precious Lord" and "Peace In the Valley."[184] Legendary African American gospel musicians were trained and mentored by Dorsey; they included Mahalia Jackson, Sallie Martin, Roberta Martin, and the Rev. James Cleveland.[185]

A few years later, after the death of his father in 1945, Tommy became a lead singer for the Staley Brothers, a local gospel quartet from Salley, South Carolina.[186] The Staley Brothers were part of the African American quartet tradition of gospel music that originated at Fisk University, an historic African American university located in Nashville, Tennessee in 1871.[187] During that year, Fisk University formed the Fisk Jubilee Singers, a student choir that went on tour to raise

---

180   Telephone conversation with Martha E. Oliver, daughter of Floster and Nora Miles Ellison.

181   Telephone conversation with Robert B. Thompson, son of R.D Thompson.

182   Telephone conversation with Martha E. Oliver.

183   Lornell, Kip, "Dorsey, Thomas (1899–1993) "Blues and Gospel Musician and Composer," The New Encyclopedia of Southern Culture Volume 12: Music, pp. 221–223.

184   Lornell, Kip, "Dorsey, Thomas (1899–1993) "Blues and Gospel Musician and Composer"

185   Lornell, Kip, "Dorsey, Thomas (1899–1993)

186   Telephone conversation with Martha E. Oliver, daughter of Floster and Nora Miles Ellison.

187   Telephone conversation with John Staley, son of Paul and Ella Holmes Staley.

money for university, which was facing financial challenges.[188] African American gospel quartets generally have four to six members, with instrumentation that allows for more voices to be added, including a lead singer. The lead singers would add personal testimonies to their music. Another characteristic among African American quartet groups is improvisation in the form of ad-libbing, dance movements, acting, and crowd participation.

The Staley Brothers included brothers Lester Staley, Sr., Matthew Staley, Eugene W. Staley, and Paul Staley, Jr., along with members Luther Evans and Bill Johnson.[189] [190] The group held performances at various venues across Aiken County, notably Gum Ridge School, Red Hill Baptist Church, and Rosa Hill Missionary Baptist Church. Their average concert attendance was between forty and fifty people, and they charged guests forty cents, sometimes higher, depending on the venue. The Staley Brothers were part of a local talent of African American gospel musicians who rose to stardom from the Wagener-Salley area, which included Louis Johnson of the legendary Swan Silvertones, Eugene Corley of the legendary Southern Six of Springfield, South Carolina, and brothers Charles Staley and Calvin Staley of the Gospel Originals.[191]

In the early 1950s, Tommy left Salley and migrated to Brooklyn, New York to be closer to his mother, paternal aunts/uncles, and seek better opportunities.[192] Tommy befriended his uncle, James Ellison, who loved music and cultivated Tommy talent. During the first few years living in Brooklyn, Tommy sang background for Madame Edna Gallman Cooke, who was a leading pioneer in gospel music. Later, Tommy joined the legendary Harmonizing Four, who were very popular and made national acclaim performing at the 1944 National Baptist Convention and President Franklin D. Roosevelt's funeral in 1945.[193] In 1955, Tommy left the Harmonizing Four and joined the Chosen Gospel Singers, one of the greatest African American jubilee quartets in the 1950s. Some of the songs Tommy recorded with the group were "Hallelujah", "This Old Soul

---

188   James, Sheire (July 1974). "National Register of Historic Places Inventory-Nomination: Fisk University—Jubilee Hall" (pdf). National Park Service.

189   Telephone conversation with John Staley, son of Paul and Ella Holmes Staley.

190   The Staley Brothers were members of Friendship Baptist Church.

191   The Gospel Originals comprised of Lester Staley, Sr. sons Charles & Calvin Staley.

192   Telephone conversation with Martha E. Oliver, daughter of Floster and Nora Miles Ellison.

193   Sacré, Robert (1974). "The Harmonizing Four," Encyclopedia of American gospel music (ed. by W. K. McNeil); Routledge Press, 2005, p. 174

"of Mine", "Troubles of the World Condition", and "Do Thy Will".[94] In 1957, the group disbanded due to a lack of work and disagreements in musical tastes.[195]

After leaving the Chosen Gospel Singers, Tommy befriended Charlie Baker, a native of Pageland, South Carolina, who owned a barber shop in Brooklyn, New York.[196] Charlie was the leader of the gospel quartet, the Five Singing Stars. Tommy began singing with the quartet and instantly became the lead singer. Upon Charlie's recommendation based on Tommy's experience, leadership and notoriety, in 1960, the group renamed itself "Tommy Ellison and the Five Singing Stars." Members of the quartet at one time or another included Charlie Baker, Billy Hardie, Dennis Bowers, Joe Dawkins Jr., Franklin "Big O" Hardnett, Justin Mickens, Joseph Ricks Horns, Sam Moses, Sam Williams, and Perry Taft. The quartet incorporated an eclectic philosophy of music with a blend of rock and roll, blues, and conviviality. Their music reflects diverse experiences and observations rooted in the Christian faith, realism, and folklore.

The Singing Stars recorded under several record labels, including Revelation, Peacock Records, HOB, HSE Records, and Atlantic International Records.[197] The quartet released a string of successful albums including "Closer," "Born Again," "Going to See My Friend," "Come Home," "Power," "Let This Be A Lesson To You," and well-known singles, including "Trying to Get to Heaven," "Pity in the City," "Let This Be A Lesson to You" (Drunk Driver), and "On My Way To Grandma House."[198] They performed across the country, started a fan club, and regularly appeared on radio and television and performed at New York City's renowned venues: Madison Square Garden, Apollo Theater, and Carnegie Hall. In 2004, the quartet was included on *Living Legends of Gospel Music, Volume 2,* narrated by the legendary Lou Rawls, who was Tommy's colleague from the Chosen Gospel Singers.[199] The group shared the stage with legendary figures in gospel music, included Shirley Caesar, Mahalia Jackson, The Swan Silvertones, The Williams Brothers, The Mighty Clouds of Joy, Doc McKenzie and The Hi-Lites, and other legendary greats.[200]

Tommy's leadership and ingenuity were the driving forces for his group's successes. Before it was time for him and his group to perform, Tommy would sit in the back of the audience to

194   In-person conversation with Tommy Ellison.

195   Tommy Ellison

196   Interview with Sammie Williams, member of "Tommy Ellison & Five Singing Stars."

197   "Tommy Ellison & The Singing Stars." Malaco Records. Accessed December 5, 2020; retrieved from https://www.malaco.com/artists/gospel/tommy-ellison-the-singing-stars/.

198   "Tommy Ellison & The Singing Stars." Malaco Records.

199   "Tommy Ellison & The Singing Stars."

200   Ibid

observe them and garner a sense of the audience's mood to determine which songs he and his group would perform.[201] In developing concepts for his songs, Tommy, along with his group, drew from their experiences and self-reflection rooted in practical life lessons, family life, societal problems, morality; in addition to uplifting harmonic songs of joy and encouragement in the Christian faith. He cultivated members' talents and showcased them during performances. Tommy, himself, led by example by encouraging members to practice self-discipline and avoid unnecessary distractions that deterred them from living a good life.

Tommy's character was charismatic, generous, and devout in nature. Tommy was very devoted to his family, especially his grandparents; his sister, Mae Hammonds Fogle; his son, Joseph Jordan; and his extended family that included the Singing Stars, friends and contemporaries in the music industry. Tommy was good friends with music legends James Brown, Shirley Caesar, Sam Cook, and even the legendary Bumpy Johnson.[202] Tommy was a role model in gospel music and advised many quartet groups and soloists. Furthermore, Tommy never forgot where he came from and was appreciative of his fans, who he considered his family. In 2002, Tommy and The Five Singing Stars were inducted into American Gospel Quartet Convention Hall of Fame, and in 2007, they received a resolution passed from the South Carolina House of Representatives recognizing the group for outstanding contributions in preserving the heritage of African American gospel music.[203]

On January 3, 2009, Tommy died in Baltimore, Maryland at the age of seventy-seven.[204] Tommy's legacy in African American gospel music needs no explanation; his work and contributions speak volumes about his greatness. But greatness is imagined with a vision and every vision has a beginning. Tommy's vision of becoming a renowned gospel artist started at home, singing on the children's church choir, and it was inspired by the voice of his grandmother to embrace gospel music. Tommy was much more than a celebratory figure. Tommy loved his family, especially his grandparents who raised him, and he never forgot where he came from. Tommy's life transcended gospel music. Tommy embraced the inherent goodness of people and their nature, which included his family, friends, and the millions of loving fans that embraced him over the years.

---

201   Interview with Harry Govan. President of Harry Govan Gospel Song Ministries.

202   Sammie Williams.

203   "Tommy Ellison & The Singing Stars." Malaco Records; retrieved from https://www.malaco.com/artists/gospel/tommy-ellison-the-singing-stars/.

204   Tommy is buried at Smyrna Missionary Baptist Church, Springfield, South Carolina

A Life Defined by Purposeful Living and Benevolent Service: The Story of Floster L. Ellison, Jr.

"Good Barber, good man to your wife, learn how to treat people with respect, take care of your family, take care of your family, take care of your neighborhood."—Floster L. Ellison, Jr.

"If you organize your life around your passion, you can turn your passion into your story and then turn your story into something bigger—something that matters"-Blake Mycoskie

"My dad is my hero."—Alvin Ellison, son of Floster L. Ellison, Jr.

Floster Leon Ellison, Jr., the son of Floster "Tan" and Nora Miles Ellison, Sr., was born in the Sawyerdale Community of western Orangeburg County on October 10, 1921.

At an early age, Floster was exposed to white collar professions who many people in his childhood were not exposed to. Floster's father was an entrepreneur who owned a syrup mill and millet grinder. Floster's mother was a professional caregiver who cared for the sick and those in need from all backgrounds. Floster was very close to his parents and his sister Thelma, who taught him the importance of having purpose in life by identifying a profession that renders service. By being exposed to family professions, Floster gained valuable experiences in sound business practices, encouraged to pursue formal education, and cultivated a spirit of benevolent service. These experiences influenced his worldview and proved invaluable later his life.

In 1937, Floster's parents relocated to the outskirts of Salley, South Carolina, where they purchased 500 acres of land. The move proved beneficial. Floster joined his family's church, Smyrna Missionary Baptist Church, where he was an active member and later ordained as a deacon under the administration of Rev. William H. Coleman.[205] Floster's father was also ordained as a deacon and served as treasurer, and his mother prepared the wine for Holy Communion and helped prepare candidates for baptism.[206] On May 31, 1941, Floster graduated from Schofield Normal and Industrial Institute, a prestigious boarding school for training African American students in industrial trades and teaching, located in Aiken, South Carolina.[207] Upon graduation, Floster moved in with his sister, Nannie Ellison Ware, who lived in Philadelphia, Pennsylvania. In Philadelphia, Floster was briefly employed as a laborer at Atlantic Refining Company, which was a local oil and petroleum company.[208]

On December 7, 1941, Japanese aircraft attacked the major US naval base at Pearl Harbor in Hawaii, taking the Americans by surprise and claiming the lives of more than 2,300 troops. The attack on Pearl Harbor resulted in Congress declaring war on Japan on December 8, 1941, resulting in the United States entering World War II. While the country was mobilizing for war, domestically, racial discrimination and segregation inhibited African Americans' mobility to achieve equality. African American leadership advocated and led efforts to desegregate public institutions that were influenced by racism. One institution African American leadership targeted was the US Navy by focusing on changing the navy's recruitment polices.[209] Consequently, on February 7, 1942, the navy announced that African Americans would be enlisted in general and messman service beginning on June 1, 1942.[210] The following year, on February 1, 1943, roughly 20,000 African American sailors were messman.[211] A few months later, on May 15, 1943, Floster enlisted in the navy and acquired the skill of barbering, which became a lifelong passion.[212]

During his military service, on July 1, 1944, Floster married Alice Marie Smith in Muskogee, Oklahoma.[213] After the war, they settled in Columbia, South Carolina and started a family. Their union was blessed with four sons: Alvin Leon Ellison, Vernon Cecil Ellison, Michael Carl Ellison, and Thaddeus Cornell Ellison. For the first few years, the family lived in the historic Waverly

---

205   Floster L. Ellison, Jr., Obituary, 2006.

206   Martha E. Oliver. "Family History." New York, n.d.

207   Schofield Normal and Industrial School Commencement Program, 1941.

208   Ancestry.com. U.S., World War II Draft Cards Young Men, 1940–1947.

209   History.Navy.mil, African Americans in General Service, 1942.

210   History.Navy.mil

211   Ibid.

212   Ancestry.com. Pennsylvania, U.S., Veteran Compensation Application Files, WWII, 1950–1966.

213   Ancestry.com. Oklahoma, U.S., County Marriage Records, 1890–1995.

community, which is designated as Columbia's first suburb.[214] Waverly was a progressive community of African Americans that included artisans, professionals, and social reformers who were instrumental in the social and political advancement of Africans Americans in Columbia and South Carolina. In 1950, the family lived in nearby Lower Waverly, a less-affluent African American neighborhood that was blighted by debris and inadequate infrastructure issues.[215] [216]

A few years after the end of World War II, Floster began his illustrious career in professional barbering. He started working at a local barbershop located in downtown Columbia, under the supervision of Mr. Smith.[217] In 1947, Floster partnered with his friend, Joseph Stroy, and they opened their own barbershop named Ellison & Stroy, located in the historic Columbia African American business district along Washington Street before the Civil Rights Movement.[218] They charged seventy-five cents for haircuts, twenty-five cents for mustache and beard grooming, and they employed barbers who they charged ten percent from their profits for rent and other expenses.[219] Their clientele was very diverse across racial and socioeconomic communities. Ellison and Stroy barbershop's also benefited from the patronage of African American businesses, educators, and civic leaders. As a professional barber, Floster incorporated moral principles and pride into his work.

During the 1950s, Floster began to progressively transform his life. He received his bachelor's degree from Benedict College in 1954 and pursued graduate studies at Clark Atlanta University a few years later, where he earned a master's degree in social work in 1960.[220] [221] [222] While at Clark Atlanta, on April 17, 1957, Floster participated in a town meeting titled "How Can Students Make the World Better?" with faculty and fellow students and wrote his master's thesis titled, *A Study of the Social Service Convalescent Program at Northville State Hospital, and Patients' Reaction to the Program.*[223]

---

214   Ancestry.com. U.S., City Directories, 1822–1995.

215   Ancestry.com. Pennsylvania, U.S., Veteran Compensation Application Files, WWII, 1950–1966.

216   HistoricColumbia.org/online-tours/lower-waverly.

217   Interview with Alvin Ellison, son of Floster Leon and Alice Marie Smith, Jr.

218   Interview with Willie Anderson, member of the Palmetto State Barbers Association.

219   Interview with Willie Anderson.

220   Floster L. Ellison, Jr., Obituary, 2006.

221   The Atlanta University Bulletin (catalogue), s. III no. 110;1959–1960; Announcements 1960–1961; retrieved from http://hdl.handle.net/20.500.12322/002.au.bulletin:0246.

222   The Atlanta University Bulletin (catalogue), s. III no. 110; 1959–1960; Announcements 1960–1961; retrieved from http://hdl.handle.net/20.500.12322/002.au.bulletin:0246.

223   The Atlanta University Bulletin (newsletter), s. III no. 103: July 1958; retrieved from http://hdl.handle.net/20.500.12322/002.au.bulletin:0104.

[224] Tired of renting, Floster and his family achieved the dream of homeownership and relocated permanently to the newly established Greenview Community, a suburb in northern Columbia that was once a cow pasture and a planned community for African American veterans like Floster, who were given opportunities to buy homes for their families. Floster opened his barbershop in the Greenview Community shopping center, in addition to several barbershops and a beauty salon.[225] In conjunction with furthering his pursuits, Floster was instrumental in the organization of Greenview First Baptist Church, where he served as a deacon and church treasurer. Floster later became the first president of Fairwold Junior High School Parents Teachers Association.[226] [227]

Floster's professional and personal activities took place during a monumental period in history known as the Civil Rights Movement. Stemming from the governmental refusal to protect the civil rights of African Americans and the immorality of racism, the movement was a series of collective action activities rooted in agitation and advocacy. South Carolina was an epicenter of the movement making national acclaim in the Briggs v. Elliot (1952) case that exposed the segregation of school buses in Clarendon County which led to the historical Supreme Court landmark case, Brown v. The Board of Education (1954) that culminated with the landmark decision that deemed segregated schools unconstitutional. In addition, Columbia was an epicenter of the movement because of its distinction as the state capital, home of three higher education institutions, and politically engaged communities. Student protesters from Allen University and Benedict College amplified their demonstrations downtown near the State House and Main Street. Local civic organizations organized demonstrations, sit-ins, and issued advocacy campaigns to push for racial and social equality.

Inspired by the activism of the Civil Rights Movement, on July 18, 1960, Floster and Luther Lilliewood, along with several others, founded the Palmetto State Barbers Association.[228] The founding purpose was to "encourage the practice of barbering as a profession and to promote ethical principles and practices therein; to increase the usefulness of the profession to the public and

---

224   Ellison, Floster L. (1959). A study of the social service convalescent program at Northville State Hospital, and the patients reaction to the program, 1959; retrieved from http://hdl.handle.net/20.500.12322/cau.td:1959_ellison_jr_floster_1

225   Interview with Alvin Ellison, son of Floster Leon and Alice Marie Smith, Jr.

226   Floster L. Ellison, Jr., Obituary, 2006.

227   Encyclopedia of schools; retrieved from https://localhistory.richlandlibrary.com/digital/collection/p-16817coll11/id/7834/rec/1

228   Certificate of Incorporation by the Secretary of State, The State of South Carolina, July 18, 1960, The Office of the Secretary of State, Columbia, South Carolina.

to create a better understanding and a more meaningful relationship among the barbers of South Carolina."[229] The association's charge was given by Floster with these encouraging words: "Barber, one who shaves and trims the beard and cuts the air. The trade of barbering is one of great antiquity." [230] The association envisioned itself as a collaborative entity, unifying licensed professional African American barbers to promote the values of professionalism, integrity, education, and service. It would become a civic organization whose members would serve the community in which they lived and work.

Floster was elected as the association's first president and served until 1970. During Floster's early tenure, the association focused on cracking down on unlicensed barbers and lobbied the state government for African American representation on the State Board of Barber Examiners. On September 11, 1963, Floster spoke before the board about the prospect of hiring an African American inspector:

> We are members of the Colored Barber Association, which is a Negro Organization, primarily, for the betterment of barber shops and for customers of these shops. About a month ago we went down and talked to the Governor in regard to getting some representation with the Board. He was very receptive of us. I was told by Mr. George Patterson that there might be a chance of getting an Inspector. Our hope at this time is to support the Barber Board. We don't have to account to any one person. We are dictated to by any outside organization or group. There are many things that we could do that you might not be able to do. Our hope is to work with you and support you. We are not trying to dictate. We are with every effort the Board puts forth. We have able to get barbers in our organization that are most interested in the barber profession. We have many violators, and we think we can be a help to the Board in locating these violators.[231]

The board was so impressed with Floster's eloquence based on his profound knowledge, they wanted to hire him as an inspector on the spot. Floster was interested in the position but wanted to confer with the association to discuss the matter before accepting the position. On October 4, 1963, Floster was hired as the first African American barber inspector in the state of South Carolina, with a salary of $17.50 per day, plus mileage and expenses.[232]

---

229 Certificate of Incorporation by the Secretary of State.

230 Palmettostatebarbersassociation.wordpress.com/about-us/.

231 State Board of Barber Examiners Minutes, August 14, 1963; retrieved from The South Carolina Department of Archives and History.

232 State Board of Barber Examiners Minutes, October 4, 1963; retrieved from The South Carolina Department of Archives and History.

Floster inspected African-American-owned barbershops and occasionally White-owned barbershops.[233] [234] It was Floster's mission during his inspections to ensure that barbers were professionally capable and qualified to do their jobs according to the law and adhere to professional standards. Floster's mission was furthered echoed during a meeting with the Master Barbers Association, an organization comprised of predominantly White barbers "to be men of honor, character and dignity" and warned "unless the barbers meet present day challenges and organized their efforts, the cause of barbering will suffer for lack of interest among young people who would go into the profession."[235] Shortly afte Floster's term ended in 1970, the association successfully lobbied the State Board of Barber Examiners for African American representation on the board, and members ran for political office in their respective communities.[236] [237] [238]

In conjunction with his flourishing barbering career, Floster was determined to succeed in the field of social work. In the early 1960s, Floster was employed as a case worker at Palmetto State Hospital, which was a mental health facility for African American patients operated by the South Carolina Department of Mental Health.[239] In the summer of 1965, Floster was promoted to Chief of Social services of the hospital Division of Social Services.[240] The *Variety*, the Palmetto State Hospital newsletter, publicly lauded Floster's efforts in improving services:

> Mr. Ellison who was recently promoted this past summer from Acting Chief to Chief of Social Service, is still running the show. To him goes the credit for recruiting our new staff members. He continues to be very active in hospital and community activities. In particular, we wish to commend his services with Waverly Social Club which as been guiding light for many ex-patients and patients who are on their way out of the hospital.[241]

---

233   Interview with Alvin Ellison, son of Floster Leon and Alice Marie Smith Ellison, Jr.

234   Interview with Willie Anderson, member of the Palmetto State Barber Association.

235   "Chief Barber Inspector Talks To Association." The Times and Democrat, May 25, 1965; retrieved from www.newspapers.com.

236   "Named to Board." The Gaffney Ledger, June 30, 1972; retrieved from www.newspapers.com.

237   "Rainey Issues Statement." The Gaffney Ledger, December 24, 1971; retrieved from www.newspapers.com.

238   "Vaugh Running for Commission." The Item, March 22, 1976; retrieved from. www.newspapers.com.

239   Floster L. Ellison, Jr., Obituary, 2006.

240   The Variety Newsletter: Vol.13, No. 10, Columbia, SC; November,1965, p.17; retrieved from www.statelibrary.sc.gov.

241   The Variety Newsletter: Vol.13, No. 10, Columbia, SC; November,1965, p.17; retrieved from www.statelibrary.sc.gov.

Floster, along with his nephew who worked under him, Otis Corbitt, successfully increased the number of African American employees at the hospital. Several **recruits** of whom were Benedict College graduates and even recruited an employee from Salley, Francis Williams, a graduate of Tuskegee University.[242]

While Floster's social work career flourished, the Palmetto State Hospital drew the ire of the Richland County Citizens Committee. The committee leader, Modjeska Simkins, who was an important leader in public health reform during the Civil Rights Movement, highlighted the deplorable conditions of the hospital.[243] In a letter to the South Carolina General Assembly, dated on January 25, 1965, the committee expressed their grievances:

> January 15, many patients were seen running through snow and sleet to and from meals in one garment—no; shoes, headgear or coats. They had to gobble in food in this condition, return to their dormitories and allow their garments to dry on their bodies. Reportedly some buildings are chilly. Most patients do not have changing apparel and none is available on wards for aids to distribute when necessary. Much clothing is age-old army surplus. Sleeping garments are unheard of—most patients sleeping in apparel worn during the day. Neither interest nor regard is a hown relative to size, color, or condition of clothing or shoes. A patient wears what can be wheedled out of the master of the supply room. Aids report that'-they are third-degreed when they request clothing. Articles necessary for personal hygiene, such as scap, toothpaste, washcloths, towels, etc., for individual patients are unheard of. It is reported that towels have not been seen in the buildings for months. In some wards a dozen washcloths must be shared by thirty patients. Ordinarily, patients bathe and dry themselves with rags sent in for janitorial purposes. If supplies in necessary quantities are delivered to the Negro asylum, wde-ducks" must have massive channels from the supply rooms to parts unknown.[244]

The committee's grievances undergirded the reasoning of the Civil Rights of Act of 1964 that required the desegregation of public facilities and provision of equitable accommodations. In 1965, the South Carolina Department of Mental Health integrated, and the former Palmetto Hospital

---

242   The Variety Newsletter: Vol.13, No. 10, Columbia, SC; November,1965, p.17; retrieved from www.statelibrary.sc.gov.

243   Modjeska Simkins Papers. Series: Topical files. South Carolina Political Collections, pp.1–2; retrieved from https://digital.tcl.sc.edu/digital/collection/mmsimkins/id/11508/rec/4.

244   Modjeska Simkins Papers. Series: Topical files. South Carolina Political Collections, pp.1–2; retrieved from https://digital.tcl.sc.edu/digital/collection/mmsimkins/id/11508/rec/4.

was renamed Crafts-Farrow State Hospital.[245] This resulted in substantial improvements within the hospital that included maintenance upgrades and reform in mental health services. Floster became the first Director of Social Services at Crafts-Farrow and served in that capacity for the next twenty years.[246] [247]

Upon his retirement from barbering and mental healthcare services, Floster spent considerable time with his loved ones and continued to serve his community. Floster was a continued presence of inspiration and wisdom. During his retirement, Floster remained active as a deacon, remained active with the Palmetto State Barbers Association, and the Ellison-Miles Family Reunion Council until his health declined. On September 18, 2006, Floster died at the age of eighty-five.[248] [249] [250]

Floster's legacy is unparalleled. Floster truly organized his passion into a story and turned his story into something that was meaningful. Floster transcended beyond being an ordinary barber to an entrepreneur in the barbering industry. Inspired by the activism of the Civil Rights Movement, Floster co-founded the Palmetto State Barbers Association to give African American barbers a professional space to collaborate, cultivate their knowledge in the barbering industry, and invigorate a spirit of advocacy to address the needs and challenges of African American barbers across South Carolina. Today, the association continues its work in hosting barber competitions, educational classes, and advocacy. In addition to his illustrious barbering career, Floster's contributions to the field of mental health in South Carolina are renowned. Floster made history as the first African American Chief of Social Services at Palmetto and Crafts-Farrow State Hospital. He instituted reforms, recruited African American employees, and became a mentor to the employees in his division included his nephew, Otis Corbitt, who later earned his PhD from Columbia University and became a high ranking offical at the South Carolina Department of Mental Health for many years.

Floster's professional successes never overshadowed his love for his family and church.

---

245 Action Council Newsletter, p.4; retrieved from http://www.crossculturalactioncouncil.org/images/pdf/2017%20Newsletter.pdf.

246 Action Council Newsletter, p.4; retrieved from http://www.crossculturalactioncouncil.org/images/pdf/2017%20Newsletter.

247 Floster L. Ellison, Jr. Obituary, 2006.

248 Floster L. Ellison, Jr. Obituary, 2006.

249 Floster, along with his wife Alice Marie, are buried at Smyrna Missionary Baptist Church, Springfield, South Carolina.

250 Floster wife, Alice Marie, died on April 21st, 2019.

251 Interview with Alvin Ellison, son Floter L. and Alice Marie Smith, Jr.

Bibliography

Action Council Newsletter, p. 4; retrieved from
http://www.crossculturalactioncouncil.org/images/pdf/2017%20Newsletter.pdf.
"Aiken County Economy." The Aiken Standard, September 30, 1975; retrieved from
www.newspapers.com.
Acts and Joint Resolutions by the Legislature-Sessions 1870 and 1871." The Edgefield
Advertiser; retrieved from www.newspapers.com.
Ancestry.com. Oklahoma, U.S., County Marriage Records, 1890–1995.
Ancestry.com. Pennsylvania, U.S., Veteran Compensation Application Files, WWII, 1950–1966.
Ancestry.com. South Carolina, County Marriage Records, 1907–2000.
Ancestry.com. South Carolina Death Records, 1821–1968.
Ancestry.com. U.S. City Directories, 1822–1995.
Ancestry.com. 1860 U.S Federal Census-Slave Schedule, H.E. Phillips.
Ancestry.com. 1910 United States Federal Census.
Ancestry.com. 1920 United States Federal Census.
Ancestry.com. 1930 United States Federal Census.
Ancestry.com. 1940 United States Federal Census.
Ancestry.com. U.S., World War I Draft Registration Cards, 1917–1918.
Ancestry.com. United States Word War II Draft Cards Young Men, 1940–1947.
Bouknight, A. N. (2010). "Casualty of Progress": The Ward One Community and Urban Renewal,
Columbia, South Carolina, 1964–1974; retrieved from

https://scholarcommons.sc.edu/etd/142.

Certificate of Incorporation by the Secretary of State, The State of South Carolina, July 18, 1960, The Office of the Secretary of State, Columbia, South Carolina.

"Chief Barber Inspector Talks To Association." The Times and Democrat, May 25, 1965. retrieved from www.newspapers.com.

Cleveland, Christina. "Aiken County Celebrates Founders Day," March 10, 2017. www.aikenstandard.com.

Deed from Alice Seawright to Ted T. Busbee, 7 November 1957 (filed 8 November 1957), Aiken County, South Carolina, Title Book No.207, p.270, Clerk of Court for Aiken County.

Ellison, Floster L. (1959). A study of the social service convalescent program at Northville State Hospital, and the patients reaction to the program, 1959; retrieved from http://hdl.handle. net/20.500.12322/cau.td:1959_ellison_jr_floster_l.

Encyclopedia of schools; retrieved from https://localhistory.richlandlibrary.com/digital/ collection/ p16817coll11/id/7834/rec

Family Search.org. Death Certificate for David Searight.

Family Search.org. Death Certificate for Martha Ellison.

FamilySearch.org, Ohio Deaths, 1908–1953.

FamilySearch.org "United States, Freedmen's Bureau Labor Contracts, Indenture and Apprenticeship Records, 1865–1872."

FamilySearch.org. 1870 United States Federal Census.

Family Search.org. 1880 United States Federal Census.

Family Search.org. 1900 United States Federal Census.

Family Search org. 1920 United States Federal Census.

Floster L. Ellison, Jr., Obituary, 2006.

Genealogy Trails History. 90 Years of Aiken County, Aiken County, South Carolina Genealogy Trails; retrieved from www.genealogytrails.com/scar/aiken/aiken_hx.htm.

"Going in Depth ~ SC Freedmen's Bureau Labor Contracts," May 21, 2015; retrieved from https://lowcountryafricana.com/going-in-depth-sc-freedmens-bureau-labor-contracts/.

Graham, Jr., Cole Blease. Constitutions. Columbia, SC: University of South Carolina, Institute for Southern Studies, 2016.

Harvey, Mary Phillips. Under the Heel of the Invader, ca. 1925., 1925.

"History, Art & Archives, U.S. House of Representatives, "The Civil Rights Bill of 1866.";
retrieved from www.history.house.gov/Historical-Highlights/1851-1900/The-Civil- Rights-Bill-of-1866/.

HistoricColumbia.org/online-tours/lower-waverly.

History.Navy.mil, African Americans in General Service, 1942.

History-The War Between the States." Accessed May 11, 2020; retrieved from http://www.williston-sc.com/history/war/.'

In-person conversation with Arthur Seawright, son of Wallace and Armenia Wooden Seawright.

In-person conversation with Catherine Seawright McCollough, daughter of Robert L. & Alice Thompson.

In-person conversation with Cheryl Seawright Curry, daughter of Wallace and Armenia Wooden Seawright.

In-person conversation with Flora Dunbar Harris, former student of Saint Paul Elementary School located in Sawyerdale.

In-person conversation with Essie Johnson Pontoo, daughter of Ocie and Essie L. Johnson.

In-person conversation with Leroy Gantt, husband of Barbra Jean Wooden Gantt.

In-person conversation with Otis Corbitt, son of John and Thelma Ellison Corbitt.

In-person conversation with Michael Seawright, son of Wilson and Nancy Johnson Seawright.

In-person conversation with Rev. Mack Staley, son of Paul and Ella Holmes Staley.

In-person conversation with Nancy Johnson Seawright, wife of Wilson Seawright.

In-person conversation with Romeo Ellison, son of Jerome and Dollie Ellison.

Interview with Willie Anderson, member of the Palmetto State Barbers Association.

Interview with Alvin Ellison, son of Floster Leon and Alice Marie Smith, Jr.

Interview with Harry Govan. President of Harry Govan Gospel Song Ministries.

Interview with Robert L. Seawright, son of Wallace and Armenia Wooden Seawright.

Interview with Sammie Williams, member of "Tommy Ellison & Five Singing Stars."

"Items for Perry." Aiken Standard, January 11, 1893; retrieved from www.newspapers.com.

James, Sheire (July 1974). "National Register of Historic Places Inventory-Nomination: Fisk University–Jubilee Hall" (pdf). National Park Service.

Jenkins, Ellen Bush and Belcher, Posey. Barnwell County. Columbia, SC: University of South Carolina, Institute for Southern Studies, 2016.

"Juneteenth Worldwide Celebration." Juneteenth Worldwide Celebration; retrieved from www.juneteenth.com.

Lornell, Kip, "Dorsey, Thomas (1899–1993) "Blues and Gospel Musician and Composer," The New Encyclopedia of Southern Culture Volume 12: Music, pp. 221–223.

Minchin, Timothy J. Black Activism, the 1964 Civil Rights Act, and the Radical Integration of the Southern Textile Industry." The Journal of Southern History 65, no.4 (1999): 809–44.

Modjeska Simkins Papers. Series: Topical files. South Carolina Political Collections, pp.1–2. retrieved from https://digital.tcl.sc.edu/digital/collection/mmsimkins/id/11508/rec/4.

Named to Board. The Gaffney Ledger, June 30, 1972; retrieved from www.newspapers.com.

"Negro Farmers Increase Soil Conservation." The Aiken Standard, July 28, 1950; retrieved from www.newspapers.com.

Palmettostatebarbersassociation.wordpress.com/about-us/.

"Rainey Issues Statement." The Gaffney Ledger, December 24, 1971; retrieved from www.newspapers.com.

"Retirements," Graniteville Bulletin, n.d.

Sacré, Robert (1974). "The Harmonizing Four," Encyclopedia of American gospel music (ed. by W. K. McNeil); Routledge Press, 2005, p. 174.

Schofield Normal and Industrial School Commencement Program, 1941.

Schmidt, James D. Freedmen's Bureau. Columbia, SC: University of South Carolina, Institute for Southern Studies, 2016.

Seilger, Robert S. South Carolina's military organizations during the War between the States. Charleston: History Press, 2008.

State Board of Barber Examiners Minutes, August 14, 1963; retrieved from The South Carolina Department of Archives and History.

State Board of Barber Examiners Minutes, October 4, 1963; retrieved from The South Carolina Department of Archives and History.

South Carolina Historical Properties Record; retrieved from www.schpr.gov.

Telephone conservation with Arthur L. Seawright, son of Wallace and Armenia Wooden Seawright.

Telephone conversation with Martha E. Oliver, daughter of Floster T. and Nora Ellison Miles.

Telephone conversation with John Staley, son of Paul and Ella Holmes Staley.

Telephone conversation with Robert B. Thompson, son of R.D. Thompson.

"Tenant Farming in the South." The Times and Democrat, March 06, 1937; retrieved from www.newspapers.com.

"Tommy Ellison & The Singing Stars." Malaco Records; retrieved from https://www.malaco.com/artists/gospel/tommy-ellison-the-singing-stars/.

The Atlanta University Bulletin (newsletter), s. III no. 103: July 1958; retrieved from http://hdl.handle.net/20.500.12322/002.au.bulletin:0104

The Atlanta University Bulletin (catalogue), s. III no. 110;1959–1960; Announcements 1960–1961; retrieved from http://hdl.handle.net/20.500.12322/002.au.bulletin:0246.

The Center of African American History, Art, and Culture (2008). A Pictorial History of African Americans in Aiken County, edited by T. Ella Strother.

The Variety Newsletter: Vol.13, No. 10, Columbia, SC; November,1965, p.17; retrieved from www.statelibrary.sc.gov.

"Vaugh Running for Commission." The Item, March 22, 1976; retrieved from. www.newspapers.com.

"Wagener Wavelets." Aiken Standard, February 17th, 1892; retrieved from www.newspapers.com.

"Where Kauri Gum Is Found." Aiken Standard, March 15, 1893; retrieved from www.newspapers.com.

Wilson, Sondra Kathryn. "Meet Me at the Theresa: The Story of Harlem's Most Famous Hotel," 2004. p. 205.

APPENDIXES

APPEDENIX I–GENERAL PICTURES

This section includes pictures of the individuals in the book, not limited to the following information:

1. Grave markers
2. Place of Residences
3. Death Certificates
4. Siblings, children, and parents of the individuals in the book
5. Picture of Piney Grove School
6. Floster L. & Alice Marie Smith Ellison, Jr. Marriage License

Joseph & Martha Kitchings Seawright Ellison, Sr.

Curtis "Kirkland" Seawright, Sr. and his wife, Annie Schofield Seawright

Curtis "Kirkland" Seawright, Sr. is the oldest son of Dave and Martha Kitchings Seawright Elli-son. Curtis and his wife Annie were blessed with eight children: Lessie Seawright Hook, Watson Seawright, Tillman Seawright, Clifford Seawright, Curtis "Ceg" Seawright, Jr., Wilson Seaw-right, David Seawright, Sr, and Martha Seawright Aiken. Curtis and his family were farmers. Curtis was a prominent bootlegger who was known for making liquor in the local area. He had no fingers on his left hand, only his thumb!

Floster "Tan" Ellison, Sr. and his wife, Nora Miles Ellison

Floster "Tan" Ellison is the oldest son of Joseph and Martha Kitchings Seawright Ellison. Floster and his wife Nora were blessed with ten children: Thelma Ellison Corbitt, Victoria Ellison, Joe Louis Ellison, Ausbon Ellison, Holly Ellison, Floster L Ellison, Jr., James Ellison, Nannie Ellison Ware, Geneva Ellison Brown, Allie Mae Zeigler Wilson, Mary Ellison, and Martha Ellison Oliver.

Joseph Ellison, Sr. Death Certificate

Source: Ancestry.com. South Carolina, U.S., Death Records, 1821-1968

Martha Kitchings Seawright Ellison Death Certificate

Source: Ancestry.com. South Carolina, U.S., Death Records, 1821-1968

Joseph & Martha Kitchings Seawright Ellison grave marker

Smyrna Missionary Baptist Church Cemetery, Springfield, South Carolina

The Family of Roosevelt Seawright

Top row from left to right: Ronald "Ronnie" Seawright, Patricia Seawright Adams, Reginald "Reggie" Seawright, Sharon Seawright Childs, Renee Seawright. **Bottom row from left to right:** Roosevelt Seawright (son of Wilson & Eliza Edwards Seawright) and his wife, Louise Jenkins Seawright.

The children of Roosevelt & Louise Jenkins Seawright

Left picture from left to right: Reginald "Reggie Seawright. Ronald "Ronnie" Seawright
Right picture, top row from left to right: Sharon Seawright Childs, Patricia Seawright Adams, Renee Seawright. **Bottom middle:** Louise Jenkins Seawright, wife of Roosevelt Seawright

Henry & Shirley McKevie Seawright

Henry is the son of Wilson & Eliza Edwards Seawright

The children of Henry and Shirley McKevie Seawright

From left to right: Michelle Seawright, Stephanie Seawright Smith, & Connie
Seawright

Wilson Seawright

Son of Curtis "Kirkland" & Annie Schofield Seawright, Sr.

Eliza Edwards Seawright

Wife of Wilson Seawright

Haskell Seawright

Son of Wilson Seawright & Beatrice Seawright Harper

Mildred Seawright Corley Patterson

Daughter of Wilson & Eliza Edwards Seawright

Martha Seawright Corbitt Minor

Daughter of Wilson & Eliza Edwards Seawright

Roosevelt Seawright grave marker

Sunset Memorial Gardens Cemetery, Graniteville, South Carolina

Henry Edward Seawright grave marker

Ashley Grove Baptist Church Cemetery, Aiken, South Carolina

Wallace Seawright, Sr., and his wife Armenia Wooden Seawright

Wallace Seawright, Sr., is the son of Robert L. & Alice Thompson Seawright

Wallace & Armenia Wooden Seawright Graves

Baughmanville Baptist Church Cemetery, Wagener, South Carolina

The sons of Wallace & Armenia Wooden Seawright, Sr.

From left to right: Robert L. Seawright, Ronnie Seawright, Gregory L. Seawright, Willie Seawright, Sr., Artis Seawright, Wallace Seawright, Jr., Roosevelt "Poke" Seawright, and Arthur L. Seawright.

The daughters of Wallace & Armenia Wooden Seawright, Sr.

From left to right: Barbara Seawright Garvin, Cheryl Seawright Curry, Alice M. Seawright, Armenia Seawright Wright, Dorothy Seawright Landy, Catherine Seawright Garvin, Annette Seawright Patterson, **and** Corine Seawright Leaphart.

Wilson Seawright

Son of Robert L. & Alice Thompson Seawright

Catherine Seawright McCollough

Daughter of Robert L. & Alice Thompson Seawright

Robert L. Seawright Death Certificate

Source: Ancestry.com. South Carolina, U.S., Death Records, 1821-1968

MRS. ALICE SEAWRIGHT

WAGENER — Mrs. Alice Seawright died Monday at Aiken County Hospital.

Mrs. Seawright was born in Aiken County, daughter of the late P u r v e s t and Francis Thompson.

Surviving are a daughter, Mrs. Catherine McClaught of Jamaica, N.Y.; and two sons, Wallace Seawright of Salley and Wilson Seawright of Jamaica, N. Y.

Funeral services will be Sunday at 1:30 p.m. in Smyrna Baptist Church, conducted by the Rev. W. L. Watson.

Robinson Funeral Home is in charge.

Alice Thompson Seawright Newspaper Obituary

"I remember when my father, Wilson Seawright, was told that his mother, Grandma Alice, was in the hospital. He went on to work, at JFK Airport, that day, and said that he will take the airplane to Columbia, SC, if she got any worse! The next day, my mother, Sadie, told him to not wait until his mother dies, then go home, to South Carolina. I remember my mother packing his clothes, in preparation for my dad, to go home! I believe, Grandma Alice died, before she saw him! I was a young girl, and if anyone knows anything different, about whether she saw my father, before she passed away, I stand corrected. My Grandma Alice babysat, for Sandy and I, when she moved to Jamaica, NY. Before my father and mother separated, she moved back to South Carolina, where she died! I never saw her husband, who was my Grandfather Robert Seawright, because he died in 1960, the same year that I was born! All three of their children, are with them, now, and all of them are resting in Paradise!!"-**Andrea Linda Roulac, daughter of Wilson Seawright**

Source: Ancestry.com. Web: Richland County, South Carolina, U.S., Obituary Index, 1892-2000

Wallace & Armenia Wooden Seawright Home

Inkberry Road
Salley, South Carolina

Friendship Baptist Church

Salley, South Carolina

Friendship Baptist Church was where Wallace met his wife, Armenia Wooden, the youngest
daughter of Harry J. and Annie Reed Wooden Bolton.

Alice Thompson Seawright lived with her son, Wilson, and his family, at 152–27 118th Avenue (the middle home), Jamaica, Queens, New York.

Alice T. Seawright lived with her sister, Lumanda Thompson Williams and her family on 126-18 147th Street, Jamacia, Queens, New York City.

Arthur Seawright grave marker

Smyrna Missionary Baptist Church Cemetery, Springfield, South Carolina

Arthur Seawright was the son of Dave and Martha Kitchings Seawright Ellison. He died on January 6th, 1911 at the age of 30. His son, Robert L. Seawright, named his son, Arthur, after his father. Robert's son, Wallace Seawright, Sr., named his son Arthur. Wallace's son, Arthur Lee Seawright, named his son Arthur Lamont Seawright.

The children and grandson of Floster T. and Nora Miles Ellison, Sr.

From left to right: James Ellison (son), Nannie Ellison Ware (daughter), Thelma Ellison Corbitt (daughter), Geneva Ellison Brown (daughter), Allie Mae Ellison Wilson Zeigler (daughter), Floster L. Ellison, Jr. (son), Martha Ellison Oliver (daughter), and Tommy Ellison (grandson)

Holly Ellison (son)

The Ellison Estates (The Home Place of Floster & Nora Miles Ellison, Sr.)

Ellison Estates Road
Salley, South Carolina
The boyhood home of Tommy Ellison aka Mr. Superstar of Gospel

Floster T. and Nora Miles Ellison, Sr. grave markers

Smyrna Missionary Baptist Church Cemetery, Springfield, South Carolina

"Mr. Superstar" of Gospel, Tommy Ellison

Piney Grove School, Salley, South Carolina

Piney Grove School was an African American elementary located between Salley and Aiken during the era of segregation. The school served students in grade 1st through 8th grade and had three rooms. **Tommy Ellison, (first person on the left in the row with students' knees on the ground) attended the school.**

Tommy Ellison with Catherine Seawright McCollough

In this picture, Tommy Ellison took a picture with Catherine Seawright McCollough, daughter of Robert L. & Alice Thompson Seawright at a concert in New York City. Catherine was a fan of Tommy music and she along with her siblings, Wallace and Wilson Seawright grew up with Tommy in Salley, South Carolina.

Tommy Ellison grave marker

Smyrna Missionary Baptist Church Cemetery, Springfield, South Carolina

Floster L & Alice Marie Smith Ellison, Jr.

Marriage License

(Valid only in Muskogee County)

STATE OF OKLAHOMA, Muskogee County   IN COUNTY COURT

To any Person Authorized to Perform the Marriage Ceremony, GREETING:

You are hereby authorized to join in marriage Mr. *Foster Leon Ellison Jr.* of *McAlister*, County of *Pittsburg*, State of *Okla*, aged *23* years,

and M. *Marie Alice Smith* of *Muskogee*, County of *Muskogee*, State of *Okla*, aged *16* years.

And of this License you will make due return to my office within thirty days from this date.

WITNESS my hand and official seal, this *30th* day of *June*, A. D. 19*44*.

Jess H. Childers   Court Clerk

(SEAL)   By *Marian Stampe*   Deputy

Recorded this *30th* day of *June*, 19*44*

Jess H. Childers   Court Clerk

By *Marian Stampe*   Deputy

Floster L. & Alice Marie Smith Ellison, Jr. Marriage License

Source: Ancestry.com. Oklahoma, U.S., County Marriage Records, 1890–1995

Floster L & Alice Marie Smith Ellison children

From left to right: Thaddeus Ellison, Alivn Ellison, Michael Ellison, and Cecil Ellison

Floster L. & Alice Marie Smith Ellison grave marker

Smyrna Missionary Baptist Church Cemetery, Springfield, South Carolina

APPENDIX II–THE FAMILY CHURCHES

This section includes information about the family churches of the Seawright-Ellison family:

1. A picture of Smyrna Missionary Baptist Church
2. A picture of Oakey Springs Missionary Baptist Church
3. A picture of Antioch Missionary Baptist Church
4. A picture of Baughmanville Baptist Church

Smyrna Missionary Baptist Church
Springfield, South Carolina

In 1873, Smyrna Missionary Baptist Church was founded. Floster T. Ellison, Sr. served as deacon and briefly as church treasurer; his wife, Nora served as deaconess; and his son, Floster L. Ellison, Jr., served as deacon. James W. Kitchings, a nephew of Martha Kitchings Seawright Ellison and Tuskegee University graduate, was elected as general manager to construct a new building for the church.

Many relatives of the Seawright, Ellison, and Kitchings family were members.

Oakey Springs Missionary Baptist Church
Salley, South Carolina

In 1870, Oakey Springs Missionary Baptist Church was founded. From 1870 until the early 1880s, the Seawright family and several relatives of the Kitchings family attended the church. Oakey Springs is the mother church of several churches in the area: Flora Branch Baptist Church, Antioch Missionary Baptist Church, Gospel Temple Baptist Church, Samaria Missionary Baptist Church, and Sardis Missionary Baptist Church.

Curtis "Kirkland" Seawright, Sr., along with his wife, Annie Schofield, and their family were members.

Antioch Missionary Baptist Church
North, South Carolina

In 1876, Antioch Missionary Baptist Church was founded. Furman Seawright, along with his wife Ella Davis, and their family were members. Furman's maternal uncle, Furman Kitchings and his wife, Carrie Schofield, and their family were members as well.

The Old Antioch Missionary Baptist Church
North, South Carolina

From 1876 until October 21, 1969, members of Antioch Missionary Baptist Church worship a the old church until October 21, 1969 when the new church was built. The old church structures still standing.

**Baughmanville Missionary Baptist Church
Wagener, South Carolina**

In 1901, Baughmanville Baptist Church in the New Holland Community, north of Wagener, South Carolina. When Robert L. Seawright along with his family moved to the New Holland Community in the mid-1930s, his son Wallace Seawright, Sr., joined the church at the age of nine. Wallace was very active in the church who served faithfully as a deacon and senior choir member.

Seven of Wallace' sons became members of Baughmanville. His sons, Wallace Seawright, Jr., and Robert L. Seawright, and grandson, Gregory Garvin, joined the church trustee board. Later several of his grandchildren and other descendants became members.

Remembering

Gladys Williams
Lois Jordan
Girlean Williams
Gussie Wright
Rev. H. P. Clark
Dea. Brigg Williams
Dea. James Frazier
Dea. Wallace Seawright, Sr.
Eddie Lou Holloway
Venus Harris
Minnie Davis
Ruth Gantt
Leathella Singleton
Dea. Howard Holloway

Senior Choir and Gospel Chorus Members

Baughmanville Missionary Baptist Church
Senior Choir and Gospel Chorus Members

Wallace Seawright, Sr. is on the far right (see Dea. Wallace Seawright, Sr.)

Source: Baughmanville Missionary Baptist Church anniversary book

Jerusalem Lodge #400 (PHA-Prince Hall Affiliated)

To further his spiritual growth, Wallace joined Prince Hall Masonic Order as a member of Jerusalem Lodge #400. He actively participated in lodge activities and formulated lifelong relationships with his fellow brethren. Wallace's uncle, Purvis "Bush" Thompson, Jr., was a member and Past Master of the lodge.

APPENDIX III–THE PHILLIPS FAMILY

During the Reconstruction era from January 1st, 1867 until January 2nd, 1868, Martha along with her father and siblings, were sharecroppers who lived and work on the Phillips Plantation near Williston, South Carolina. The plantation owner was Hugh E. Phillips, a former slaveowner and son of a Revolutionary War veteran. Hugh's wife, Keziah Antionette Willis, whose family the town of Williston was named after.

This section includes the following information:

1. Mary Phillips Harvey, the daughter of Hugh E. and Keziah Willis Phillips, account, "Under the Heels of the Invader", that details the destruction of Williston by Union troops during the Civil War including how her father life and slaves were threatened by the troops.
2. Pictures of Hugh E. Phillips, Keziah Antionette Willis Phillips, and Mary Phillips Harvey
3. An image of the Original Phillips Plantation Map
4. A picture of the Ashley-Willis House
5. Pictures of grave markers of Hugh E. Phillips, Keziah Antionette Willis Phillips, and Mary Phillips Harvey

Hugh E. & Keziah Antionette Willis Phillips

Mary Phillips Harvey

Contributor: Courtesy of Carol McCiver, descendant of Hugh E. & Keziah Antionette Willis Phillips

The Original Phillips Plantation Map

The picture of the map is the location of Hugh E. Phillips plantation which covered the north section of the town of Williston to the South Edisto River boundaries to the Orangeburg and Aiken County lines. The two main roads of the Phillips Plantation were present day Hwy 39 (from Orangeburg County crossing into Barnwell County and Davis Bridge Road (from Aiken County crossing into Barnwell County). The plantation included a slave cemetery and a dam.

Contributor: Carol McCiver, descendant of Hugh E. & Keziah Antionette Willis Phillps

Written by Mary Keziah Phillips Harvey, daughter of Hugh Edward Phillips and Keziah Willis, when she was in her 80s. Their home was in Williston, S.C.

RECOLLECTIONS OF THE WAR BETWEEN THE STATES BY A SCHOOLGIRL

UNDER THE HEELS OF THE INVADER

My recollections of the war between the States are those of a schoolgirl. Brought up in a typical Southern home, I had seen only the sunny side of life. When my elders began discussing Secession, and possible war, their tones, and words were made on my mind. They often remarked that IF we had war, it would be of only a few months duration, and the the South would be independent. It is a matter of history that South Carolina was the first state to secede, then others followed in quick succession. The young men formed themselves into companies, and when picnics were given, they were the guests of honor. The flags were flying, drums beating, and we were a merry crowd. When the good-byes were spoken, the soldier boys assured their friends that they would soon return victorious.

About this time, I was sent to school in Columbia, and at rare intervals we saw soldiers, sometimes home on furlough, and sometimes, one with an empty sleeve, which told its own story or war! During my vacations, I noticed a growing anxiety, and the papers were eagerly scanned for news from the front.
Sh! we began to realize what was meant, for none of us knew how soon we might see the names of some of our own loved ones among the lists of wounded, captured, or killed.

As time went on our soldiers needed more clothing than the government could supply, and hundreds of boxes were sent by private individuals. We (the young girls) were anxious to help, so we learned to knit socks for our soldier boys, and we sang "Dixie," "Maryland, My Maryland," "Bonnie Blue Flag," "When This Cruel War is Over," and other patriotic songs, while we worked. The older ladies decided that on certain days they would bring food to give to the soldiers as they passed through our town on the trains. The men who were well enough came out to a table filled with good things to eat, for our ladies were always eager to give to the soldiers--the BEST. Some of the poor fellows were too sick to leave the cars, so a few of the ladies went to those, with well-filled trays, until all were served, and as the trains moved off, hats were waved, and many lips repeated, "God bless you ladies!"

The horizon was darkening, but my father told us that the South would NEVER be conquered -- and it never was! It was only overpowered by numbers. The last year of my college life, Confederate money had depreciated in value so much that we girls would pay five dollars for a small package of candy, the same amount for a yard of calico - if we could find the calico! Many of the stores were closed, and the few which

"Under the Heels of the Invader"
Written by Mary Phillips Harvey

96

were open were dependent upon blockade runners for goods. Coffee and sugar were becoming very scarce, and expensive, as well as a great many other things. Flour must have been scarce also, for I remember that during my last year at school, we were given a great deal of cornbread. We learned to braid palmetto to make our hats, which we trimmed with rosetts of the same material. New ribbons, and flowers were not to be had at any price.

As dress goods became more, and more scarce, the people learned to weave very pretty homespun, which looked very much like the ginghams of today. I was very proud indeed of my first homespun dress.

By that time the hospitals were full to overflowing, and as soon as the sick or wounded soldiers were able to travel, they were sent away, and private families took them in, and cared for them gladly, until they were able to return to the front, for we were helping in that way our beloved South.

When my parents heard that Sherman's army was coming to South Carolina, they decided that it would be unsafe for me to remain at home, as they had heard wild rumors of the treatment of Southern girls by Northern soldiers. A neighbor near us also had a daughter whom he was anxious to send to a place of safety. After a consultation, they decided to send us to Augusta, so we went on the LAST train which passed over this road before it was torn up by Sherman's men. While there, we saw a few Yankee prisoners which were taken during a skirmish near Aiken. We remained three weeks in Augusta, then my friend's brother was sent for us and he told us that we would find many sad changes. Instead of a carriage he brought a wagon drawn by two poor horses, which had probably been discarded as worthless, by Sherman's soldiers. I can never forget the sight which met my eyes on my return!!

My home was in ruins--a mass of brick and ashes. The flower yard trampled by the feet of many horses, and pieces of my piano scattered around. Some kind-hearted soldiers, (for some were kind) saved it from the flames, only to be broken in pieces by others. Some even cut the wires out with an axe, and gave them to some poor people who lived near us, and the made knitting needles of it.

My mother told me that my father followed the soldiers around in the house trying to keep them from burning it. They would open a closet door, and throw coals of fire inside. Several times my father put it out, then the soldiers surrounded him, and putting pistols to his head, told him that if he did not desist they would kill him. My mother begged him to let it burn, for she saw that if he persisted in trying to save it, he would be murdered before her eyes.

The servants were threatened with death if they did not tell where the silver was buried, but they could not tell what they did not know. My father was told that he would be killed unless he gave up the gold which they believed he had hidden, but the gold they wanted he did not have, for his absolute faith in the ultimate independence of the South made him quite content with the Confederate stocks and bonds, and which, alas, he

"Under the Heels of the Invader" (con't)

afterwards found so useless! The curbing and buckets at the well were burned, and that night when my mother and little brother (the only ones at home) were suffering from thirst, my father unintentionally got into the enemies lines as he was going to a neighbor's well. He was taken prisoner, and kept for hours, while my mother was in an agony of fear, not knowing what had befallen him.

After our home was burned, my parents moved into one of the negro houses, where they were at least sheltered from the cold, for my father had comfortable houses for his slaves. The one opposite we used as a cook and dining room. Our food was of the plainest, and not very abundant. We ate with wooden spoons, for it was unsafe to use the silver, on account of stragglers who followed the army, so it remained buried for a long time. Some of the slaves were faithful, but others left, and we never saw them again. Day after day the returning soldiers passed our door foot sore, and weary. Many of them with pieces of old shoes tied with strings. How different from the homecoming which they planned when they left us, so full of hope, and so confident of success!!

It was hard to see my mother (who had always been accustomed to trained servants) trying to do work for which she was physically unfitted, but the women of the South were brave. "While the war lasted, they made heroic sacrifices, and when the cause they loved so well was lost, they took up their added burdens uncomplainingly. The South they had loved in all her pride, was no more, but in her desolation, she was dearer than ever before. The story of ruined homes, and broken hearts, of suffering, and want, in a country made desolate!"

"Let us obey the Divine command to forgive; let us forget its horrors if we can, and remember only that it was shown the world to what sublime heights the soul of our people could rise in time of distress and sorrow."

(signed) Mrs. H.J. Harvey

Compliments of Carol Phillips Mciver

(760) 688-8047

cpmciver@yahoo.com

"Under the Heels of the Invader" (con't)

The Ashley-Willis House

The Ashley Willis House is a Greek revival house was built between 1833 and 1850 and features a wide gable- front form unusual for the period. John Ashley and then Elijah Willis owned this land before 1850: the house was likely built by the Ashley family. Williston, chartered in 1858, was named for the Willis family, which gave land for a depot on the S.C. Rail Road, for a church (now First Baptist Church), and for a school. Elijah was the paternal uncle of Keziah Antionette Willis, wife of Hugh E. Phillips.

The town's oldest house occupies a prominent location between the S.C. Rail Road and the Augusta Charleston Road. As W.T. Sherman's Federal army advanced through the area on February 8-9, 1865, Gen. Judson Kilpatrick used this house as his headquarters before burning most of the town and proceeding to Aiken and Columbia. The house was listed in the National Register of Historic Places in 2004.

Source: The Ashley-Willis house - Williston, South Carolina. (n.d.). Retrieved March 14, 2021, from http://ashleywillishouse.com/

Hugh E. Phillips grave marker

Rocky Swamp United Methodist Church Cemetery, Neeses, South Carolina

Keziah Willis Antionette grave marker

Rocky Swamp United Methodist Church Cemetery, Neeses, South Carolina

APPENDIX IV–Juneteenth & The Freedmen Labor Contract

Juneteenth, also known as Juneteenth Independence Day or Freedom Day, is a holiday that commemorates June 19th, 1865, announcement of the abolishment of chattel slavery in the state of Texas, and more generally the emancipation of enslaved African Americans throughout the United States. After the Civil War, the federal government created the Freedmen's Bureau. The bureau created and administered the freedmen's labor contracts for freedmen and Whites as well.

This section includes:

1. "General Orders, No. 3" newspaper article
2. The original and transcribed freedmen labor contract signed between Hugh E. Phillips & The Kitchings family that included Martha Kitchings Seawright Ellison.

HEADQUARTERS DISTRICT OF TEXAS,
GALVESTON TEXAS, June 19, 1865.

General Orders, No. 3.

The people are informed that, in accordance with a proclamation from the Executive of the United States, all slaves are free. This involves an absolute equality of personal rights and rights of property, between former masters and slaves, and the connection heretofore existing between them, becomes that between employer and hired labor.— The Freedmen are advised to remain at their present homes, and work for wages. They are informed that they will not be allowed to collect at military posts; and that they will not be supported in idleness either there or elsewhere.   By order of

Major-General GRANGER.

(Signed,)   F. W. EMERY, Maj. & A. A. G.

"General Orders, No. 3", The Galveston Daily News, June 19th, 1865

General Orders, No. 3 symbolizes the historical significance of Juneteenth, celebrated annually on June 19th in African American and diverse communities across the country. Texas was the last Confederate state to free their slaves, due to the fact that the news of federal emancipation of slaves didn't reach Texas until June 19th, 1865 when Union troops lead by Major General Gordon Granger landed in Galveston, Texas.

Source: https://www.newspapers.com/clip/75322735/juneteeth1865/

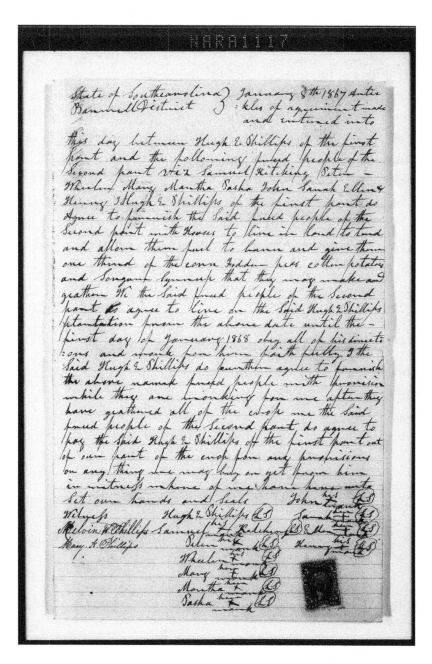

The Original Freedmen Labor Contract Source:
FamilySearch.org "'United States, Freedmen's Bureau Labor Contracts, Indenture and Apprenticeship Records, 1865–1872."

State of South Carolina   }

Barnwell District} January 8th, 1867 Articles of agreement made and entered into this day between Hugh E. Phillips of the first part and the following freed people of the Second part viz Samuel Kitching, Peter, Wheeler, Mary, Martha, Pasha, John, Sarah, Ellen, & Henry. I Hugh E. Phillips of the first part do Agree to furnish the Said freed people of the Second part with Houses to live in, land to tend and allow them fuel to burn and give them one third of the corn, Fodder, peas, cotton, potatoes and Sorghum Syrup that they may make and gather. We the Said freed people of the Second part do agree to live on the Said Hugh E. Phillips plantation from the above date until the first day of January 1868, obey all his directions and work for him faithfully. I the Said Hugh E. Phillips do further agree to furnish the above named freed people with provisions while they are working for me. After they have gathered all of the crop we the Said freed people of the Second part do agree to pay the Said Hugh E. Phillips of the first part out of our part of the crop for any provisions on any thing we may buy or get from him in witness where of we have unto Set our hands and Seals

Witness
Hugh E. Phillips (LS)★   John (his X mark) (LS)
Melvin W. Phillips   Samuel (his X mark) Kitchens (LS)
Mary K. Phillips   Sarah (her X mark) (LS)
                                   Peter (his X mark) (LS)
                                   Ellen (her X mark) (LS)
                                   Wheeler (his X mark) (LS)
                                   Henry (his X mark) (LS)
                                   Mary (her X mark) (LS)
                                   Martha (her X mark) (LS)
                                   Pasha (her X mark) (LS)

★(LS) stands for Legal Signature

The transcription of the original freedmen's labor contract
This document is transcribed verbatim apart from punctuation to make it easier to read and understand. The document was transcribed by Tonya Browder, genealogist of the Old Edgefield District Genealogical Society.

APPENDIX V–THE FOUNDING OF
AIKEN COUNTY & THE HAMBURG MASSACRE

On March 10, 1871, African American men Prince Rivers, Charles D. Haynes, Samuel J. Lee, William B. Jones, and others founded Aiken County, which is the only county founded by African Americans in South Carolina, according to records during Reconstruction. The county was named after William Aiken, the first president of the South Carolina Railroad and Canal Company. The county was formed from parts of Barnwell, Lexington, Orangeburg, and Edgefield counties. The Orangeburg County section taken to form Aiken County was northward from the North Edisto River to the south toward Tinker's Creek, where the Seawright family lived since 1870. Therefore, the Seawright family is designated as one of the first families of Aiken County.

On July 4, 1876, the town of Hamburg, a market town mostly populated by African Americans in western Aiken County near Augusta, Georgia, was the center of a key event that was known as the Hamburg Massacre. The massacre was a major civil disturbance that was planned and executed by white Democrats with the goal of suppressing African American voting in the 1876 gubernatorial election. They disrupted Republican meetings and suppressed African American civil rights through violence and intimidation. The massacre resulted in the deaths of four African American men and one white man. About ninety-four white men were indicted, but none were prosecuted. The news of the Hamburg Massacre sent shock waves throughout Aiken County, South Carolina, and nationally.

This section includes:
1. The history of the Founding of Aiken County
2. A picture of the Founders of Aiken County
3. The history of the Hamburg Massacre written by Wayne O'Bryant.
4. A newspaper article of the Hamburg Massacre

The history of the Founding of Aiken County

Samuel J. Lee served in the Confederate Army. An account in South Carolina Encyclopedia, at age sixteen, Lee accompanied Samuel J. McGowan in the Civil War, and he said that he was wounded at Second Manassas in 1862 and again near Hanover Junction in 1864. While there is no official record of Lee's service in the Confederate army, he was photographed with McGowan's regiment armed and in uniform. After the war, Lee farmed in Abbeville and soon entered politics. He served on the Edgefield County commission in 1868. That same year he was elected to the General Assembly, where he represented Edgefield County from 1868 to 1871 and Aiken County from 1872 to 1874. In 1872 Lee became the first African American elected Speaker of the South Carolina House of Representatives and later relocated to Charleston and went on to become the state most successful African American lawyers.

According to Isabel Vandervelde's book, "Aiken County: The Only South Carolina County Founded During Reconstruction," which was published in 1999, a freedman named Charles D. Haynes was conscripted and joined the Confederate army as a private in company B, 32nd Georgia Regiment under Col. Georgia P. Harrison, commanding. After the war, Hayes served in the Legislature and went on to become Aiken postmaster.

Prince Rivers served in the Union Army. Born a slave in the coastal town of Beaufort, Prince Rivers had training as an artisan and was frequently hired out by his owners as a coachman. He learned to read and write despite the legal and customary barriers to slave literacy. Following the Union occupation of Beaufort in November 1861, Rivers's white owners, the Stuart family, fled to the upcountry district of Edgefield. Making use of the dislocations of war, Rivers escaped Edgefield for the safety of Union lines on the coast. There he joined the First South Carolina Volunteers, one of the first African American Union regiments, reorganized later in the war as the Thirty-third U.S. Colored Troops.

In 1871, during the height of Reconstruction, Samuel J. Lee, Prince Rivers, and Charles D. Haynes jointed together with the assistance of others founded Aiken County: from parts of Barnwell, Edgefield, Lexington, and Orangeburg Counties. The county is named for William Aiken, first president of the South Carolina Canal and Railroad Company. As of date, Aiken County is the only South Carolina county founded by African Americans, remarkably veterans of the Civil War who were unified.

Source: www.scencyclopedia.org

The Founders of Aiken County

From left to right: Samuel J Lee, Prince Rivers, Charles D. Haynes
Source: Aiken County Historical Museum

The history of the Hamburg Massacre

Written by Wayne O'Bryant

As the nation's centennial was approaching, former Confederate soldiers from Edgefield County were devising schemes that they hoped would allow them to wrestle control of the state from "Negro Rule". The initial target was Hamburg. On July 4th, 1876, two white men, Tommy Butler and Henry Getzen attempted to drive their horse drawn buggy thru the formation of the Black militia who were drilling in the center of Market Street in Hamburg. The altercation resulted in words being exchanged but the militia eventually opened ranks and let them thru. Butler's father, Robert Butler, hired former Confederate General Mathew Butler (no relation) as his lawyer to swear out a complaint against the militia.

When Gen. Butler demanded that the militia's guns, they refuse and all hell broke loose. A mob of several hundred White men had gathered in Hamburg throughout the day. Two dozen Black militia men had taken cover in their armory when the firing began. The mob even employed a cannon in the attack. By the end of the night, two Black men and one White man had been killed and a few dozen Black men were taken captive. What happened next would go down in history as "The Hamburg Massacre". The White mob began to take unarmed Black men out of the ring of men who encircled them, and one by one began to execute them. After killing four men, some in the mob called for the killing to stop. The remaining prisoners were released and told to run. As the fled, a final volley of shots was fired into the fleeing crowd wounding some, one later died bring the final death toll to eight (one White and seven Black).

After the Hamburg Massacre, White rifle clubs united under the banner of "The Red Shirts" and unleashed a reign of terror across the State. They attacked Black citizens throughout the months leading up to the November elections. On Election Day, armed White men manned the polls to keep Black men from voting and in some counties ballot boxes were stuffed resulting in thousands more votes than there were voters. The steal would prove to be successful. Yet, in the fog of the contested SC election, a deal was being struck in the presidential election. South Carolina promised to give their electoral votes to Rutherford B. Hayes, giving him the Presidency, if he would in turn remove Federal Troops out of the South, thus ending Reconstruction. Hayes was losing the popular vote in South Carolina, so he made the deal. South Carolina delivered the winning electoral votes and Hayes kept his end of the bargain. With Federal troops withdrawn, the era of Reconstruction was over, those who lost power after the war were back in power, and Americans of African descent were stripped of their Civil Rights including their precious right to vote. The death of Reconstruction ushered in the Jim Crow Era. Within one short decade, the flame of the American Ideal, that all men were created equal, had been lit and extinguished!

THE HAMBURG MASSACRE.

RESULT OF THE CORONER'S INQUEST—SEVEN PERSONS FOUND GUILTY OF MURDER—GEN. BUTLER AMONG THE NUMBER.

CHARLESTON, Aug. 2.—The Coroner's jury in the Hamburg case find seven persons guilty of murder, namely : E. J. Butler, Henry Getson, Thomas Butler, Harrison Butler, John Lamar, Thomas Oliver, and John Oliver. They find that Moses Parks was killed by E. J. Butler ; James Cook by Henry Getsen, Thomas Butler, and Harrison Butler ; and A. T. Attoway, Daniel Phillips, Hamp Stevens, and Albert Minyard were killed by John Lamar, Thomas Oliver, and John Oliver. They find that forty-four citizens of Aiken County, S. C.; thirteen of Edgefield County, S. C., and thirty Georgians were accessories before the fact. Among the accessories from Aiken are two colored men, and from Edgefield Gen. M. C. Butler. The warrants are expected to issue to-day, and bail to any amount is ready.

The Hamburg Massacre newspaper article

In this article, references the actors involved in the Hamburg Massacre that resulted in the murder of several African American and former Confederate General M.C Butler involvement in the event.

Source: https://csidixie.org/chronicles/hamburg-massacre

APPENDIX VI–THE FOUNDING OF SALLEY, SOUTH CAROLINA

The 1880 Federal Census record show the Seawright family lived in the Rocky Grove Township of Aiken County where they continued to farm. The township was the settlement for the town of Salley founded on December 19th, 1887, named after Dempsey H. Salley, who was a state legislator responsible for incorporating the town and responsible for the railroad coming through town. The town was formed on a 1,000 acres plantation owned by Salley himself.

This section includes:

1. "Salley and The Railroad: newspaper article
2. A picture of Eli Salley
3. A picture of the original Blackville, Alston, and Newberry Road track
4. A picture of Sardis Missionary Baptist Church
5. A picture of Salley Baptist Church
6. A picture of the Captain Dempsey H. Salley grave marker
7. A picture of the Railroad Cargo Platform

Salley And The Railroad

By DOROTHY K. MacDOWELL

Salley is located upon land formerly granted to the Salley family, prior to 1800, and the town is named for this prominent family but the town of Salley was actually founded by the late Capt. Dempsey Hammond Salley.

Before 1880, a railroad to run from Blackville to the kaolin mines near Seivern was discussed from time to time, but it was 1885 before final plans toward this end were made.

The legislature granted a charter to the Blackville, Alston, and Newberry Railroad Co. Early in 1886, its board of directors was organized. George A. Wagener of Charleston was elected president. Vice presidents were Mike Brown of Blackville, Capt. Dempsey Hammond Salley, and W. W. Duncan. Gordon Gardner of Augusta surveyed the railroad from Blackville to Salley.

With the coming of the railroad, the town of Salley was incorporated by a special act of the legislature on Dec. 19, 1887. Captain Salley was a member of the legislature at that time and was instrumental in having Springfield, as well as Salley, chartered the same day.

The first train came to Salley from Blackville on Dec. 24, 1887. From 90 Years In Aiken County we get a description of the group on the train. "Capt. Dempsey Salley, founder and vice president, borrowed, from the S.C. Railroad Co., an old engine, a baggage car and one passenger car, with Jim Keene, as engineer; Eli Salley, colored, as fireman; Capt. W. W. Woodward, as conductor; Jack Scott, as baggage master, and Pat Donohue, as brakeman, the rails began humming.

"Among the first passengers were George A. Wagener, president of the company, Mike Brown, Col. Duncan, Winton Walker and John Whaley, all being stockholders in the company."

Salley and The Railroad newspaper article

Notable residents included residents who were employees at the Blackville, Alston and Newberry Railroad Company that came to Salley on December 24, 1887 which included an African American name Eli Salley (second person on the picture on the top right middle) who was a fireman. Eli was slave on the Salley Plantation owned by the town founder. According to the family history, Eli died in a railroad accident on the Charleston–Hamburg Railroad line before 1900.

Contributor: Courtesy of Gregory Harris, descendant of Eli Salley and family historian of the African American descendants of the Salley family.

Eli Salley (person on the right)

Eli Salley is one of the direct ancestors of the African American descendants of the Salley family who currently live in the Salley area and up north. The 1880 census record show that Eli Salley was living next to John Martin Salley, Sr., a white landowner. Eli married Mary Salley and they had three children: Edward Salley, Chloe Salley, and Carrie Salley.

Contributor: Courtesy of Gregory Harris, descendant of Eli Salley and family historian of the African American descendants of the Salley family.

The original Blackville, Alston, and Newberry Railroad track

The Blackville, Alston, and Newberry Railroad track ran from Blackville, South Carolina to the kaolin mines in Seivern, South Carolina. The trains were used to transport kaolin from Seivern to Blackville. The first train came to Salley from Blackville on December 24, 1887.

Sardis Missionary Baptist Church

In 1876, founded by local African Americans, Sardis Missionary Baptist Church was the first and oldest established church in the town of Salley. Nancy J. Seawright, wife of Wilson Seawright, and her children are members of the church. Nancy sons, Michael Seawright, appointed as associate minister of the church and Willie Albert Seawright appointed as church trustee.

Salley Baptist Church

Salley Baptist Church was founded in 1888. The new church was constructed in 1915.
Source: http://nationalregister.sc.gov/aiken/S10817702032/index.htm.

Captain Dempsey Salley grave marker
Salley Family Cemetery
Salley, South Carolina

Salley Railroad Cargo Platform

Constructed in 1910

Source: http://nationalregister.sc.gov/aiken/S10817702032/index.htm

APPENDIX VII–Ulysses Kitchings, Principal of Sardis School

In 1925, Sardis also built a school for African American children that was designated as Rosenwald School, named Sardis School, which was headquartered at Sardis Missionary Baptist Church in Salley, South Carolina. Ulysses Kitchings, son of Furman and Carrie Schofield Kitchings and nephew of Martha Kitchings Seawright Ellison, was a principal and superintendent of the school, along with his wife, Annie Lou, who also taught at the school.

This section includes the following newspapers articles documenting notable events during Ulysses tenure at Sardis School:

1. "School Notes"
2. "Of This And That"
3. "Community Day at the Colored School"
4. "Salley Colored School Closes"
5. "Salley Negro School to Close"

School Notes

The ground has been turned for the fall community garden and it will be planted ater the next rain. Educational pictures and news of the day reels were shown to the pupils of the school last Wednesday. This is a fine idea and permits many children to "enjoy while they learn," that that find it impossible to attend the night shows. Many of the lower grades have enrolled for 4-H work—the upper grades are already well organized. The first issue of the school paper, Hi-Notes, will be off the press in a few days. The Negro school opened Thursday morning with a large enrollment. Ulysses Kitchings is again serving as principal. —

"School Notes", Aiken Standard, October 19, 1938
Source: https://www.newspapers.com/clip/73355218/sardis-school-ulysses-kitchings/

We regret that there are three more vacancies in the Salley school, (white) two for department work and one for the first grade. In the colored school, Mrs. Mary Frances Williams, who has taught here for some years has resigned to accept a school at Springfield which is her home town. The other two teachers at the colored school have been reelected and are Ulysses Kitchings, Supeirntendent, his wife, Annie Lou Kitchings and Juanita Johnston.——

Colored school closed last week with attractive exercises. On the first night, an operetta was given by the smaller children and on the second night, the older students gave a play. A special guest at the festivities was Clyde Blassingale, superintendent of Union Academy.

"Of This And That", Aiken Standard, May 29th, 1940
Source: https://www.newspapers.com/clip/73355384/sardis-school-ulysses-kitchings/

Community Day At Colored School

A community day program was given at the Sardis (Colored) school, Salley, Saturday, February 22. The program consisted of two parts.

The following schools were represented: Union Academy, Perry; Wagener, Piney Grove, Gum Ridge, Springfield and Varnville from Hampton County.

"Community Day at Colored School", Aiken Standard, March 7th, 1941
Source: https://www.newspapers.com/clip/73587141/community-day-at-colored-school-ulysses/

Salley Colored School Closes

The graduation exercises of the Salley Colored school started Sunday when the Baccalaureate sermon was preached by the Rev. E. E. Taylor, of Columbia, at Sardis Baptist Church.

Monday being Registration Day there were no exercises but on Tuesday night, the primary grades gave their contribution to the closing festivities.

The commencement exercises were held Thursday night in the school Auditorium. The program was as follows:

Prayer, Supt. Bellinger of Perry School; Salutatory, Reba Lyles; Oration, "What We Owe Our Parents," Marie Gleaton; Valedictory, "In Lighter Vein," Pintha Ree Ware.

The graduating address was delivered by the Rev. Bruce Williamson, who received his education in Virginia and England.

The guest speaker was Justine W. Washington, Jean Teacher, Aiken.

The graduates were Lela Bee Cobb, Reba Lyles, Clara Singleton, Pintha Ree Ware, Esther Dunbar, Marie Gleaton, Esther Anna Ware.

Among the white folks present were Miss Dora Ashley, Miss Lois Dicks and Miss Neta Dicks.

The Principal of the school Ulysses Kitchings, and teachers Juanita Johnson, Ira R. Ballinger and Anna Lou Kitchings, have been re-elected for the coming term.

"Salley Colored School Closes", Aiken Standard, May 2, 1942

Source: https://www.newspapers.com/clip/73354923/ulysses-kitchings-salley-colored/

Salley Negro School To Close

On Monday night the closing exercises will begin with a play and recitations by the first grade, Juanita J. Carson, teacher. An operetta entitled "Awakening of Spring" will be presented by the 2nd and 3rd grades, Annie L. Kitchens, teacher.

gan their commencement exercises Sunday afternoon, May 2nd, with the Baccalaureate sermon preached by the Rev. J. B. Hammond, principal of Piney Grove school.

On Tuesday night the 4th and 5th grades will present a play entitled "Object Matrimony" which will be directed by their teacher, Ira J. Bellinger.

Wednesday night, the graduating exercises will be held with the address being given by Prof. R. A. Merritt, principal of Varnville school, Varnville. The following features will be presented:

Salutatory with Oration—"Onward and Upward"—Flora Mae Walker.

Oration—"Shall We Advance or Shall We Stand Still"—Evernesa Louise Ware.

Valedictory with Oration—"A Broader Vision"—John C. Walker.

The commencement exercises will be under the supervision of U. S. Kitchens who has been superintendent of Sardis school for many years and to whom goes much of the credit for the fine school building and the splendid student record.

"Salley Negro School To Close", Aiken Standard, May 7th, 1943

Source: https://www.newspapers.com/clip/73586489/ulysees-kitchings-sardis-school/

APPENDIX VIII–The era of the turpentine industry in Wagener–Perry–Salley communities in the late 1800s.

The economic perils in the late 1800s encouraged Aiken County to develop new industries. In the county's eastern section, which included Salley and the new towns of Wagener, Perry, and Seivern, turpentine became a rich resource that created new industries that spurred economic growth. Perry was a bustling center for turpentine dealers.

The turpentine industry boom in the Eastern Aiken County area opened employment opportunities that attracted people to migrate there. A debonair freedman from Bennettsville, South Carolina, named Joseph Ellison Sr., relocated to Salley. He was employed as a pine tree surveyor for a local turpentine company.

This section includes the following newspaper articles that reference the turpentine industry in the area:

1. "Wagener Wavelets"
2. "Items for Perry"
3. "Where Kauri Gum Is Found"

Mr Manuel Busbee and Mr Rich have bought Mr Crawford's turpentine distillery, and have secured a quantity of the best timber in the surrounding country. Their operations will be conducted on a very extensive scale.

"Wagener Wavelets", Aiken Standard, February 17th, 1892
Source: https://www.newspapers.com/clip/50843211/wagener-wavelets-aiken-standard

For the last four or five years the lumber and turpentine dealers have done well at Perry, and they are still at work there. Mr. J. J. Keeffe is now running a still assisted by Mr. W. H. Cason as stiller.

"Items For Perry", Aiken Standard, January 11th, 1893
Source: https://www.newspapers.com/clip/73735409/items-for-perry-turpentine/

Where Kauri Gum Is Found.
Kauri gum is formed of the turpentine that has exuded from the kauri tree, a species of pine which is the finest and for general purposes the most useful forest tree in New Zealand. Thirty years ago the Maoris were the only people who employed themselves in searching for this gum, which at that time was to be found on or cropping out of the surface of the ground, where perhaps ages before forests of kauri had stood.
After a few years' exports the Maoris

"Where Kauri Gum is Found", Aiken Standard, March 13th, 1893
Source: https://www.newspapers.com/clip/50843459/where-kauri-gum-is-found-aiken/

APPENDIX IX–THE CORBETT FAMILY

After the death of his mother, Robert L. Seawright and his siblings were in the care of their paternal and maternal families. He and his brother, Gadsden, lived with their paternal uncle, Furman Seawright, and his family in Sawyerdale, located in western Orangeburg County. They lived on the property owned by John H. Corbett, Sr., who was one of Sawyerdales' leading citizens and respectable farmers. The Corbett family briefly employed the services of Furman's brother, Curtis "Kirkland" Seawright, Sr., and his wife, Annie, who also stayed on the Corbett property.

This section includes:

1. A picture of the John H. Corbett, Sr. and his family
2. An image of Furman Seawright World War 1 draft registration record
3. "Citizen Says Rocky Grove Township is Neglected In Matter of Roads"-op-ed column written by Benjamin F. Corbett, son of John H. and Frances Whetstone Corbett, Sr.
4. ""Two Townships Heard From"-op-ed column written by Johh H. Corbett, Jr., son of John H. and Frances Whestone Corbett, Sr.
5. "Sawyerdale Dots Are Chronicled" newspaper article
6. A picture Rocky Grove Baptist Church
7. John H. and Frances W. Corbett, Sr. Obituaries
8. Pictures of John H. & Frances Whestone Corbett grave markers

John H. Corbett, Sr. and his family

This picture was taken on the property of John. H Corbett which was 3 1/2 east of Salley, SC on the right of Hwy 394 when you cross into Orangeburg County from Salley. **Front row-from left to right:** Robert Elliot Corbett, John H. Corbett, Jr., **John H. Corbett, Sr.,** Florence Ellenton Corbett, **Frances Whetstone Corbett** (wife of John H. Corbett, Sr.), Benjamin Frank Corbett (in mothers lap), Sam (friend of the family). **Second row-from left to right:** Julia Corbett, George Ollen Corbett, Mary Corbett, Oscar S. Corbett. **Third row-**Curtis "Kirkland" Seawright, Sr., and Annie Schofield Seawright, African American employees of the property.

Contributor-Courtesy of Janett Corbett, descendant of John H. and Frances Whetstone Corbett, Sr.

Furman Seawright World War 1 Draft Registration Record

This draft record confirms Furman Seawright and his family who lived on John H. Corbett, Sr. property. Furman was also an employee of Corbett.

Source: Ancestry.com. U.S., World War I Draft Registration Cards, 1917-1918

Citizen Says Rocky Grove Township is Neglected in Matter of Roads

Editor Times & Democrat,
Orangeburg, S. C.

Dear Sir:—Will you please to give space through the medium of your paper for the mutual expressing of our outraged feelings and neglected rights.

We, as citizens and taxpayers of Rocky Grove township and community and as supposed residents of Orangeburg county, wish to convey to the public notice (and to the Orangeburg County Highway Commission) (though it it should be a well known fact to them,) the outrageous and neglected manner in which we of this Sawyerdale section, have treated in regards to our public roads and state highways.

Though for a long time we have realized that the officials of Orangeburg county are seemingly not aware that we too are a part of the county (at least taxpayers and voters in it, and entitled to a voice and hearing and good roads.

Judging from this long and often forgotten campaign pledge, and their long neglect of their duties, to our just rights and deserts it should be a well known fact to the officials of Orangeburg county. Unless they have destroyed all records of Rocky Grove township and marked us off their list, as apparently they have, that we have long been imposed upon and neglected, in the matter of our public roads.

Though long knowing that we have been forgotten by our official electorate, yet have we been living in hope, but seeing that all is useless, we are now raising the cry of a people in despair. It is to be remembered that a number of years back when this section was threatening of joining Aiken county in order to get good roads that certain promises in the way of good roads were made to us if we did not form a new county or join on to Aiken. Which promises have not been kept or any attempt made to fulfill them. It has now been something like 12 years since the chain gangs have visited our township, in fact it has been so long since they were seen ple, but do expect a 50.50 basis for our tax money as compared with the rest of the county. They are even taking the gangs and cutting and building new roads entirely where roads were unknown before. Yet we of Rocky Grove township fail to even get our old and muchly traveled public roads worked.

The people of the Sawyerdale section of Rocky Grove township, if desirous of going to the county seat in order to derive any benefit from the good roads, have to go by way of Aiken county through Perry, Salley, Springfield and Neeses thence on to Orangeburg, a route that covers about 40 or more miles, making it about twice as far, as it is only some 22 or 23 miles from the Sawyerdale section by way of the old 96 road. This is a very unjust imposition on our section as we are also tax payers and certainly entitled to some returns for our money. We know that we are justified in demanding that our county commissioners connect the old 96 road from Neeses on to the Aiken county line, a distance of (10) ten short miles, thereby giving the people of the Sawyerdale section some returns for their tax money and letting them also reap some benefit of the good roads, then they would be connected on to the good roads of the Aiken county line to Perry, Wagener, Salley and Springfield. We do not know of any other 10 mile stretch of road in the state that would serve the public so well as the 10 mile of the old 96 from Neeses to the Aiken county line, though possibly not so well versed in the matter of needed roads as our county commissioners. We are demanding and expecting that the Orangeburg County officials will connect this part of the 96 on from Neeses on to the Aiken county line. Where the good roads immediately commences there has long been rumors of this section joining on to Aiken county, and unless we get the square deal that is our by right, this threat will eventually be executed. The people are be-

---

**"Citizen Says Rocky Grove Township is Neglected In Matter of Roads",
Times and Democrat, August 25, 1923.**

This op-ed column written by Benjamin F. Corbett, son of John H. and Frances Whetstone Corbett, Sr criticizing Orangeburg county government for neglecting the roads in the Rocky Grove Township which included the Sawyerdale community. In the article, Benjamin reiterated a past proposition from section citizens that called for Rocky Grove township to join Aiken County to get good roads, in addition, proposed that the county connect the old 96 from Neeses, South Carolina to the Aiken County line. The old 96 road today is South Carolina State Hwy 389 that runs from Neeses through Sawyerdale into Aiken County, ending in Perry, South Carolina.

Source: https://www.newspapers.com/clip/73739483/bf-corbett-citizen-says-rocky-grove/

around here that the parents of 12 and 14 year old children are compelled to carry them (the children) to Aiken and other adjoining counties that they might see and know what a gang looks like (a most deplorable condition.) During all this time we have been living under the promises of good roads. While the gangs have been operating in and around Orangeburg most conspicuously, giving them tip top roads, while this part of the county has been solely neglected, altogether.

Take our main public roads, the old Ninety-six and Blackville road two of as important roads as are in the county, it has been something like 12 years since the gangs visited them, and then only just a little work there, and there that hardly lasted until they got back to Orangeburg, where they headed for while all these years that the gangs were working around Orangeburg, their poorest roads were in much better shape than the very best that we had. And then the good road movement with State Highways come on again. We were led to believe that the old land mark roads and the two most important in the county or state by reasons of serving the most people and being the most direct routes would be made state highways, but again we were disillusioned. Instead, they came to Neeses by 96 then to Springfield, Salley and Wagener, a most circuitous route, leaving the old 96 in sand and gutters.

Again we had hopes of the old Blackville road, but it now seems that again we are to be fooled, as every prediction points to them carrying it by Woodford, North, Livingston, Neeses, Norway, Denmark and Olar, through a section of the county that is already lined and served with good roads and highways. Why doesn't the state and county commissioners do justice and put these highways where they would serve the most people as a whole and benefit the rural sections as well as the towns, instead of just joining and linking together every little old town, so that the town folks can just jump in cars and race from one town to another. While the people of the rural districts have to put up with our deep and sand gutted roads, with all of our heavy hauling of farm produce etc. to and fro. We maintain that one section of a county is entitled to just as good roads as the rest and certainly we are not getting it, they are failing to give us a square and fair deal. We are not an envious peo-

ginning to say that our county can't give us good roads and a square deal that they will join on to a county that can. Take the map as carried in the state's issue of Aug. 4, giving the condition of our roads and highways and cutting proposed routes and you will find that there is no other township covering near the proportions of Rocky Grove township that is not served by the good roads. The only thing that we can boast of is that we have the largest territory of unworked roads in the state and unless some reader will infer that we have only two public roads, I wish to state that the 96 and Blackville roads are not our only public roads, though to look at them you would think that they were. However we have some 8 or 10 all unworked and needy.

We have a scope of country ranging in something like 20 miles long and 15 miles of unworked roads. We have no roads to North or Neeses, Springfield, Salley, Norway, Livingston, Swansea or anywhere else for that matter. It is an old and sane saying in this section, that you can tell the Aiken county line the moment you cross it, by the differences in their good roads compared to Orangeburg's poor ones, they are uniformally worked and kept in good condition. It is to be hoped by the voters and tax payers of this section, that the county commissioners will take heed of our warning and voice our sentiments among themselves and the State Highway Commissioners at their next meeting and see to it that the routing of state project No. 1 follows out the old Blackville road as well as to seeing to our need for connecting the 96 from Neeses to the Aiken county line. Also to the improving of our other public roads. We know that it takes time but we have been discriminated against all these years and are now expecting something done in short order.

We are counting on our friend, J. W. Smoak and his colleagues, and it is to be hoped that they will see our just need and rights and take steps accordingly—ere we, the citizens of this section, take the matter into our own hands. There is a remedy and one that we will avail ourselves of, unless our officials see to it that we get justice and equal rights with other sections of the county.

Respectfully,
B. F. Corbett

Salley, Aug. 24.

**"Citizen Says Rocky Grove Township is Neglected In Matter of Roads",
Times and Democrat, August 25, 1923 (con't)**

Source: https://www.newspapers.com/clip/73739483/bf-corbett-citizen-says-rocky-grove/

TWO TOWNSHIPS HEARD FROM

Writer Asks Why His Locality is Neglected by Supervisors.

Bally, R. F. D. 1, Jan. 6, 1916.
Editors The Times and Democrat:

In your issue of Tuesday, January 4, there appeared an annual report of the work done and, of the condition of our chain gangs No. 1, 2, and 3, respectively, for the year 1915.

A statement not only vouched, to be approximate and as near correct as possible, but very significant on the part of our supervisors.

We note distinctively there were fourteen townships visited during the year. Also, that some townships got a greater ratio of work done than others. While the condition of roads, of causeways and bridges in the remaining townships was things of the obsolete class, so far as our supervisors having or showing any interest in them.

We fail to see the justice of such a course, and feign would ask:

First, is the condition of public highways in Orange and a few other townships in so much need of repair and, of such importance to the people in general, as to justify the expenditure of all the road taxes, within their confines?

Second, are the roads, bridges and general conditions of such permanency in Rocky Grove Hebron and other townships as to be considered things absolute, complete?

Third, if the area of Orangeburg county be greater than it is possible to cover systematically with the force we have, what complaint have you in our drawing a line, separating the upper and neglected part from the lower and attended one? Thus, establishing a medium through which we, the ignored, can arbitrate mutually our own affairs?

Surely the supervisors must know, at least, it is their business to know, that we taxpayers of Rocky Grove and Hebron townships hold receipts against surtax collector, but as yet have received but little, if any, returns on our investment.

We are not envious of our sister townships' good road and bridges, but we believe in the religion of equality—the kind that gives some attention to each and all. Will the supervisors please inform us gently what disposition has been made of our road taxes, and if still on hand, when have we the right to use them? Isn't there an act somewhere that distinctly states that taxes shall be expended within the territory from which they were gathered? Also, inform us if the county is not divided into sections, each gang supposed to work so many till each township shall have been served? If so, why have gangs No. 1, 2, and 3 each worked in Orange township to the neglect of others? Certainly, the supervisors entrusted with our interest do not think this, the upper portion depopulated or ceased trafficking. For it has not been long since that the Aiken county gang worked a piece of road in Rocky Grove township to its expense, or should have been paid for with that township funds, yet I see no mention of same in the annual report.

Kindly advise whether the chain gang is maintained by taxation or not? If not, how is our taxes used? and when can we hope for improved roads in these parts? Seemingly, this is the time above all others for action, and we shall be greatly disappointed if our legislature do not enact or have enacted a law whereby each township shall be recognized, at least, to the extent of taxes collected therefrom, and imposing a penalty upon the party or parties in power for not exercising all of its clauses.

Trusting to see all sections given a square deal in this, the new year, as well as seeing the burial of all strife and turmoil, I am, in hoping for better road conditions.

John H. Corbett, Jr.

"Two Townships Heard From", The Times and Democrat, January 11, 1916

In this op-ed column, John H. Corbett, Jr., lambasted Orangeburg County supervisors for neglecting Rocky Grove township transportation needs and called for the legislature to recognize townships according to taxes collected and impose a penalty upon party or parties in power for not using township taxes to address transportation needs.

Source: https://www.newspapers.com/clip/75143662/two-townships-heard-from-the-times-and/

132

Sawyerdale Dots Are Chronicled

Sawyerdale, Aug. 10.—John H. Corbett, Jr., and Mrs. Mary C. Young of Sawyerdale and Mrs. Florence C. Langston and Miss Emma Young of Orangeburg attended the campaign meeting at Springfield.

Mr. and Mrs. J. L. Young and children of Norway and John H. Corbett Jr., of Sawyerdale enjoyed a three days motor trip thru Georgia last week.

John H. Corbett, Jr., and his brother Oscar and two sisters Mrs Florence C. Langston of Orangeburg and Mrs. Mary C. Young of Sawyerdale and Miss Ennover Young of Orangeburg and Miss Emily Corbett of Salley, visited in Columbia Saturday.

Mrs. J. H. Corbett Sr., Mrs. Mary C Young of Sawyerdale and Mrs. Florence C. Langston and Miss Ennover Young of Orangeburg and Miss Emily Corbett of Salley, visited Mr. and Mrs. R. E. Corbett of Pelion last week.

Mr. and Mrs. J. H. Corbett, Sr., entertained the following guests at dinner Sunday: Mr. and Mrs. J. N. Finley and Mr. and Mrs. Richard Ross all of Columbia and Mr. and Mrs. B. B. Corbett and Misses Beatrice and Alice Corbett of Neeses and Mr. D. K. Gantt and Miss Donnie Bird Corbett of Wagener.

Mr. George Weeks and Mr. G. O. Corbett and two children of Salley, Mr. and Mrs. William M Bryce of North, Mr. Hood Peele and daughter of Woodford, and Mr. and Mrs. Ernest Richardson and family of Wagener visited Mr. and Mrs. J. H. Corbett, Sr., Sunday afternoon.

Mrs. Florence C. Langston and Miss Ennoree Young of Orangeburg and Miss Emily Corbett of Salley are visiting relatives in Wagener.

Sawyerdale, Aug. 10—Mr. and Mrs. Wesley Tindal and Mrs. Joe Fogle made a trip to Columbia recently.

Miss Vesta Brown is at home after a visit to her grandparents at Woodford.

Miss Lou Belle Corbett spent a week recently with Mrs. Wesley Tindal and attended the Corinth meeting.

"Sawywerdale Dots Are Chronicled", Times and Democrat, August 14th, 1928

According Janett Corbett, on Sunday afternoon, John H. Corbett, Sr. frequently entertain guests and host dinners. Friends and neighbors from the local communities and out of town visited the Corbett family. The two articles reference the guests that John H. Corbett, Sr. entertained.

Source: https://www.newspapers.com/clip/67017959/saywerdale-dots-are-chronicled-john-h/

Rocky Grove Baptist Church
Salley, South Carolina

Rocky Grove Baptist Church is the family church of John. H. Corbett, Sr. The church was founded in 1812.

Source: http://www.rockygrovebaptistchurch.org/aboutrgbc.html

John H. Corbett, Sr. Died Friday Night

Funeral Services To Be Held This Afternoon For Prominent Farmer

Salley, April 10.—John H. Corbett, Sr., for years one of the leading citizens of this section and an outstanding farmer died here at nine o'clock tonight, after an illness of about one week. He was 79 years of age and had been in splendid health until last Saturday.

Funeral services will be held Saturday afternoon at 4 o'clock, conducted by his pastor, Rev. L. Shealey, of Pelion. Mr. Corbett was a member of the Rocky Grove Baptist church and interment will take place at the Salley cemetery.

Mr. Corbett is survived by his widow, who was Miss Frances Whetstone, and seven children: Mrs. Florence Langston, of Orangeburg; Mrs. J. L. Young, of Norway; Mrs. Mary Young, of Salley; Elliott Corbett, of Gainesville, Fla.; Oscar Corbett, Ollie Corbett and John H. Corbett, Jr., of Salley.

SAWYERDALE, Dec. 27. —Mrs. Frances M. Corbett, 89, died at her home in the Sawyerdale section, of this county, Sunday night, at 11 o'clock.

Funeral services will be conducted at 4 o'clock Tuesday afternoon from the Salley Cemetery in charge of the Rev. L. W. Shealy of Pelion, assisted by the Rev. H. C. Hester. Interment will be in the family plot.

Mrs. Corbett was widow of John H. Corbett and before marriage was Miss Frances Whetstone, daughter of the late Samuel and Martha Anne Whetstone. She was a member of the Rocky Grove Baptist church.

Mrs. Corbett is survived by three daughters, Mrs. Mary C. Young, Salley; Mrs. J. O. Young, Norway; Mrs. Florence Langston, Columbia; and four sons: G. O. Corbett, O. S. Corbett and John H. Corbett, all of Salley, and R. E. Corbett, of West Columbia. Also surviving is one sister, Mrs. B. B. Corbett, of Neeses, and one brother, C. T. Whetstone, Salley. Twenty-four grandchildren and twelve great-grandchildren also survive.

John H. and Frances W. Corbett, Sr. Obituaries

The Times and Democrat, April 11th, 1931

Source: https://www.newspapers.com/clip/51561540/john-h-corbitt-obituary

The Times and Democrat, December 28, 1943

Source: https://www.newspapers.com/clip/51613204/frances-corbitt-obituary

John H. and Frances W. Corbett, Sr. grave markers
Salley Oakview Cemetery
Salley, South Carolina

APPENDIX X–THE WARD ONE COMMUNITY

While living in Columbia, Robert L. Seawright stayed with his brother Gadsden, who lived in the historic Ward One community, which was home to many African Americans as early as the Reconstruction period. The community attracted many rural residents like Robert, who were looking for urban work to escape farming life and plentiful recreational amenities. The community had its own cultural identity reflected in entrepreneurialism, educational institutions, and bustling churches.

This section includes:

1. The history of the Ward One Community
2. Pictures of Ward One Community
3. An image of Robert L. Seawright Ward One Address Record

The history of Ward One Community

The Ward One story still is very much an open sore in Columbia's history, with many black residents still bitter about what they consider the razing of a thriving community in the name of urban renewal. Ward One was a displaced community existed between present day Pickens, Gervais, Heyward and Huger Streets in downtown Columbia. Hundreds of houses, shops and businesses covered the Ward One area from Main Street to Huger Street, and Gervais Street to east of Blossom Street.

The historic Neighborhood once included proud, humble and loving people; numerous homes & rentals, churches, schools, banks, and black-owned businesses, which has since been demolished under the guise of so labeled "urban renewal and USC's expansion". Beginning in the late 1960s through the 1980s, black residents lost their elementary and high schools in Ward One and homes, churches, and businesses. Roberson said one of the worst chapters in the memories of Ward One residents, is that city leaders condemned their community as blighted to justify their actions in overtaking the neighborhood. And many of the former Ward One residents want nothing further to do with the area. The area now is largely controlled by the University of South Carolina.

Source: "Memories flood Old Palmetto Compress Warehouse Tour"
https://www.thestate.com/news/local/civil-rights/article13842851.html.
Source: "History, A Forgotten Community Speaks" https://wardone.wixsite.com/wardone/history.

Greene Street Market

Ward One Community
Columbia, South Carolina

Neighborhood Row Houses

Ward One Community
Columbia, South Carolina

400 Park Street
Ward One Community
Columbia, South Carolina

Park Street located in the historic Ward One Community in Columbia, South Carolina. Robert frequently hung out on this street during the time he stayed there. His daughter, Catherine, saw him walking the streets and told her, "Baby I work on Park Street. I parked the car and walk the streets all day".

Source: https://wardone.wixsite.com/wardone/history.

Seawright Abr atndt VAF
" Annie r1324 Henderson
" David lab r1324 Henderson
" Ellis (Louise) lab r1121 Laurens
" Gadson (Mamie) lab h rear 526 (2)
    Sumter
" Katie maid h1324 Henderson
" Louise lndrywkr Cola Lndry & Dry
    Clnrs r1121 Laurens
" Rebecca r1013 Heidt
" Robt lab r rear 526 (2) Sumter

Robert L. Seawright Ward One Community Address

Columbia, South Carolina

In this record Robert address is **"Robt lab r rear 526 (2) Sumter"** which is present day Sumter Street, which go through the University of South Carolina campus, downtown Columbia. He lived with his brother, Gadsden Seawright and his wife, Mamie. Gadsden address is the same as Robert, **"Gadson (Mamie) lab h rear 526 (2) Sumter.**

Source: Ancestry.com. U.S., City Directories, 1822-1995.

APPENDIX XI–Pacific Mills

On December 7, 1941, Japanese aircraft attacked the major US naval base at Pearl Harbor in Hawaii, taking the Americans by surprise and claiming the lives of more than 2,300 troops. The attack on Pearl Harbor resulted in Congress declaring war on Japan on December 8, 1941 and the United States entering World War II. The war effort required production of necessities such as clothing for troops; this led to an industrialization boom across the country that created jobs. Southern urban cities, such as Columbia, South Carolina, had mills that produced cloth that prospered during the war and employed thousands of people. In early 1942, Robert L. Seawright moved to Columbia and was employed at Pacific Mills as a laborer. Pacific Mills produced 350 million yards of fabric for the war effort, which made uniforms, shirts, shorts, sheets, mattress covers, raincoats, and camouflage items.

This section includes:

1. The history of Pacific Mills
2. A picture of Pacific Mills
3. An image of Robert Seawright World War II Draft Registration Card confirming his employment at Pacific Mills.
4. A picture of Pacific Mills workers

The history of Pacific Mills

Pacific Mills began in Lawrence, Massachusetts, in 1850. After steady success, the company found that it could not weave enough cloth to keep its printing machines and bleaching kiers, or tubs, busy. To get more cloth, Pacific expanded into the South in 1915 by buying four of the sixteen mills of the financially distressed and South Carolina–based Parker Mills.

The new mills, collectively called Columbia Pacific Mills, consisted of Olympia, Granby, Richland, and Capital City Mills in Columbia. Mill villages containing 650 houses came with the purchase. In 1923 Pacific bought 750 acres of land eleven miles from Spartanburg to open Lyman Pacific Mills and another company town. The Columbia operations produced gray cloth that was shipped to Lyman or Lawrence for printing, dyeing, bleaching, and finishing. The Olympia mill had the distinction of having the largest spinning room in the world in the 1920s, with 100,320 spindles. Such massive operations made Pacific into the world's largest manufacturer of percale, a medium-weight, plain-woven printed cotton commonly used in bedsheets.

During World War II, Pacific's South Carolina mills turned out more than 350 million yards of fabric for the war effort. This cotton cloth made millions of uniforms, shirts, shorts, sheets, mattress covers, raincoats, and camouflage items. In 1954 Burlington Industries bought the entire Pacific Mills chain but retained the label because Columbia had established a reputation for high-quality bedsheets, pillow cases, and towels. M. Lowenstein & Sons bought the mills in 1955, however, and removed the Pacific name. The new owners closed the Capital City and Richland mills in 1975 and 1981, respectively. Springs Industries acquired Lowenstein in 1985 and continued to operate the Olympia and Granby mills until 1996, when the aging plants were closed.

Source: www.scencyclopedia.org/sce/entries/pacific-mills/.

Pacific Mills

510 and 600 Heyward Street
Columbia, South Carolina

Source: www.scencyclopedia.org/sce/entries/pacific-mills/.

Image of Robert L. Seawright World War II Draft Registration Card

This record confirms Robert's employment at Pacific Mills under the section **"Place of Employment or Business"**.

Source: Ancestry.com. U.S., World War II Draft Cards Young Men, 1940-1947

Pacific Mills Workers

Source: Ward One Historical Community Panel Exhibit hosted by the historical Ward One organization

APPENDIX XII–THE GOOD SAMARITAN– WAVERLY HOSPITAL

Nine days before her death on October 29, 1959, Nora M. Ellison was a patient at the Good Samaritan-Waverly Hospital where she died. The hospital which was established in 1938 and served the African American community in Columbia and the Midlands for 35 years.

This section includes:

1. The history of Good Samaritan-Waverly Hospital
2. A picture of the Good Samaritan-Waverly Hospital & Nurses
3. A picture of Dr. Matilda Evans, first South Carolina African American female physician and her home
4. A death certificate of Nora M. Ellison that document her as a patient at the Good Samaritan-Waverly Hospital.

The history of Good Samaritan-Waverly Hospital

Established in 1938 by the merger of two older hospitals, Good Samaritan-Waverly Hospital (GSWH) served the Black community in Columbia and surrounding counties for 35 years. It merged Good Samaritan Hospital, founded in 1910 by Dr. William S. Rhodes and his wife, Lillian, and Waverly Hospital, founded in 1924 by Dr. Norman A. Jenkins and his four brothers. By the mid-1930s the Duke Endowment and the Rosenwald Fund recommended a merger of the two hospitals to improve the quality of health care. After over a decade of community action and fundraising, GSWH officially opened in 1952 and operated as a segregated facility.

Black professionals, many of whom resided in the historic Waverly neighborhood, raised funds to sustain the institution. The modern, independent facility served as one of the only training facilities built exclusively for Black nurses in the city and boasted a pharmacy, laboratory, X-ray room, staff dining room, two operating rooms, and fifty beds.

Unfortunately, GSWH struggled under massive debt. City and county hospitals routinely outsourced Black patients to GSWH and refused reimbursement for treatment. As a result, there was no money available to maintain the facility or modernize its equipment.

Ironically, the passage of the Civil Rights Act and the integration of Columbia's medical facilities sealed the hospital's fate. GSWH struggled to attract white patients to keep its eligibility for Medicare funding. The integrated Richland Memorial Hospital, built in 1972, siphoned its remaining Black patient base. Good Samaritan-Waverly Hospital closed in 1973.

Source: https://greenbookofsc.com/locations/good-samaritan-waverly-hospital/.

Good Samaritan–Waverly Hospital
220 Hampton Street
Columbia, South Carolina 29202
Source: http://schpr.sc.gov/index.php/Detail/properties/12912

Good Samaritan–Waverly Hospital Nurses
Nurses pose on the steps of the Good Samaritan–Waverly Hospital
Source: https://www.historiccolumbia.org/online-tours/waverly/2204–hampton–street

Dr. Matilda Evans, first South Carolina African American female physician

Before the Good Samaritan-Waverly Hospital was established, the first African American hospital in Columbia was opened in 1901 by Dr. Matilda Evans, a native of Aiken, South Carolina and graduate of Schofield Normal and Industrial School. Evans opened the Taylor Lane Hospital in her home (see picture on the left, located on 2027 Taylor Street, Columbia, South Carolina) until she was able to finance the acquisition of a separate building for the hospital. Evans also trained nurses and partnered with white doctors who donated their services to the hospital. Funding for the Taylor Lane Hospital came from philanthropic northerners and business owners, as most patients were unable to pay for their treatments. The Taylor Lane Hospital burned in 1914.

Dr. Evans and Nora M. Ellison are related. Dr. Evans grandfather, Harry Corley and Nora's grandmother Nancy Corley Pope were half siblings. Harry and Nancy sister, Lavinia Corley Thompson, is the ancestor of the author of this book. Lavinia, Harry, and Nancy mother, Phyliss Corley, was slave from Africa. According to Lavinia oral account during her enslaved his experience to her grandchildren, she said that her mother came over her on a boat from Africa.

Source: http://www.nationalregister.sc.gov/richland/S10817740143/S10817740143.pdf

Source: The Thompson Family: Untold Stories From the Past (1830-1960)

Nora M. Ellison Death Certificate

On the death certificate section, "Full name of hospital or institution" states "Good Samaritan Waverly".

Source: Ancestry.com. South Carolina, Death Records, 1821–1968.

APPENDIX XII– THE HARLEM RENAISSANCE & HOTEL THERESA

When Tommy Ellison was a toddler, his parents moved to New York City and settled in Harlem during the height of the Harlem Renaissance, a blossoming era of African American culture in the creative arts and literature. Harlem was the symbolic capital of the cultural awakening of African Americans across the country. The Renaissance gave creative space through the arts and literature to address African American culture, civil rights, and social justice issues.

While living in Harlem, Tommy's father, Aubson Ellison, was employed at the famous Hotel Theresa, a thirteen-story hotel with 300 guest rooms. It was the largest hotel in Harlem and one of the few hotels in New York City that welcomed African American guests. The hotel hosted many prominent American figures and foreign dignitaries and was a meeting place that birthed racial justice and social movements.

This section includes:
1. Images of the Harlem Renaissance
2. The history of Hotel Theresa
3. A picture of Hotel Theresa
4. A picture of Aubson Ellison and
5. Image of his World War II Draft Registration card that documents his employment at Hotel Theresa and residence in Harlem.
6. Picture of Ausbon Ellison residence

Images of the Harlem Renaissance

Night clubs were places of pleasure for African Americans during the Harlem Renaissance. Clubs were places where they enjoyed music and swing dancing in a pleasant environment.

Source: https://allthatsinteresting.com/harlem-renaissance#12

The "world famous" Apollo Theatre established in 1923 at 253 West 125th Street in Harlem. It was a significant venue for African Americans during the Harlem Renaissance.

Source: https://www.pinterest.com/pin/570198002822792344/

Images of the Harlem Renaissance

On March 19, 1935, a race riot broke out in Harlem. After a young Puerto Rican boy was stopped for stealing from a predominately white department store, police were called but the store owners decided not to press charges. Police led him away through the back exit of the store but when he disappeared with a cop, the gathered crowd assumed he would beat the boy. The rumors spread until people believed he had been killed by police, although no harm had come to him.

Source: https://allthatsinteresting.com/harlem–renaissance#24

Images of the Harlem Renaissance

Though this incident sparked the riot, Harlem had reached a boiling point dealing with increasingly difficult living conditions. Harlem residents had long been feeling resentment over police brutality and an unemployment crisis in the neighborhood -- around 50% of people in living were out of work. Though the riots only lasted one day, three people were killed, hundreds more injured and looting and destruction of property caused $200 million dollars in damages.

Source: https://allthatsinteresting.com/harlem-renaissance#25

Images of the Harlem Renaissance

In 1935, Fitzgerald joined male vocalist Charlie Linton (left) as a singer in the Chick Webb Orchestra. Within a few years, she emerged as the group's lead singer.

Ella Fitzgerald **(lady pictured on the right)** was a popular gifted and jazz singer during the Harlem Renaissance. She won thirteen Grammys and sold ten of millions of albums. She was known the beauty and versatility of her voice and catered to people from all backgrounds. Ella has a South Carolina connection. According to research conducted by local author and historian Wayne O'Bryant, his great uncle Charles Linton of Cheraw, South Carolina **(male pictured on the left)** was male vocalist who discovered Fitzgerald. Linton was so impressed with Fitzgerald that he rented a room to get her off the streets to join his group, the Chick Webb Band.

In the 1930s and 40s, Fitzgerald frequently performed at Palmetto Park Pond and Park in North Augusta, South Carolina. The place was a recreational place for African Americans during the Jim Crow era, but featured African American performers that included Louis Armstrong, Cab Calloway, and a host of others. Whites also patronize the place as well. During the performances, there was a reserved dancing section for Whites.

Contributor: Wayne O' Bryant, local author & historian

Contributor: https://www.postandcourier.com/northaugustastar/news/

Charles Linton **(man pictured behind Fitzgerald)** was so impressed with Fitzgerald that he rented a room to get her off the streets to join his group, the Chick Webb Band. Charles and Ella fronted the Chick Webb Band until World War II, when Charles got drafted and the band broke up.

Contributor-Wayne O'Bryant, local author and historian

Images of the Harlem Renaissance

Langston Hughes is arguably the most prominent and decorated figure of the Harlem Renaissance. His writing focused on the working class experiences of African Americans, both denouncing racism and celebrating African American identity in its diverse forms. Hughes incorporated jazz rhythms into his poetry. He was a member of Omega Psi Phi Fraternity, Inc.

Zora Neale Hurston was one of the most prominent and decorated figures of the Harlem Renaissance. Her writing focused on creating unique characters that observe folks that were left out of the traditional New Negro narrative. By creating multidimensional characters about those who lived in during post slavery and poverty, Hurston work shed light on the intersectionality of the New Negro identity that were otherwise excluded from the conversation. She was a member of Zeta Phi Beta Sorority, Inc.

The history of Hotel Theresa

The Hotel Theresa, built from 1912 to 1913, has been one of the major social centers of Harlem. Serving from 1940 until its the late 1960s, when it was converted into office use, it was one of the most important community institutions for African Americans. The New York City hotel is also a noted work of the accomplished architectural firm of George and Edward Blum, and exemplifies the firm's singular approach to ornamentation and inventive use of terra cotta. Although planned primarily as an apartment hotel, the Theresa also welcomed traveling guests for short stays. In addition, the hotel contained a two-story dining room used for banquets, weddings, meetings and other functions, and a bar and grill that became a major gathering place for Harlem's black celebrities.

During the 1940s and 1950s, the Theresa was known as the "Waldorf of Harlem," playing host to many of America's most prominent black social, political, entertainment and sports figures, as well as to many foreign dignitaries. The Theresa was also home to important Harlem institutions, including the March Community Bookstore and Malcolm X's Organization of Afro-American Unity. The Theresa entered the national limelight in 1960 when Cuban premier Fidel Castro chose to stay at the hotel while visiting New York to speak at the United Nations General Assembly; while at the Theresa, Castro hosted a visit from Soviet premier Nikita Khrushchev. Encompassing the entire western block front of Adam Clayton Powell, Jr. Boulevard, between W. 124th and W. 125th streets, the Theresa is one of the most visually striking buildings in northern Manhattan. The Hotel Theresa was listed in the National Register of Historic Places on June 16, 2005.

Source: https://www.nps.gov/nr/feature/afam/2006/theresa.ht

Hotel Theresa

2082-96 Adam Clayton Powell Between West 124th and 125th Streets
Harlem Community
New York City, New York

Ausbon Ellison

Ausbon Ellison was the oldest son of Floster T and Nora Miles Ellison and father of Tommy El-lison. In this picture, Ausbon wore a Zoot suit and a brimmed hat, customed of men like Aubson who were Harlemites (residents of Harlem) during the Harlem Renaissance.

Image of Ausbon Ellison World War II draft registration card

This record confirms Aubson employment at Hotel Theresa under the section **"Place of Employment or Business"**

Source: Ancestry.com. U.S., World War II Draft Cards Young Men, 1940-1947

40-42 W 127th St

Aubson Ellison Residence
40-42 W 127th Street
Harlem Community
New York City, New York

APPENDIX XIV– SCHOFIELD NORMAL AND INDUSTRIAL SCHOOL

On May 31, 1941, Floster L. Ellison, Jr. graduated from Schofield Normal and Industrial Institute, a prestigious boarding school for training African American students in industrial trades and teaching, located in Aiken, South Carolina.

This section includes:

1. A history of Schofield Normal and Industrial School

2. Pictures of Schofield Normal and Industrial School which includes building, staff, and students.

3. An image of Schofield Normal and Industrial School 1941 commencement program documenting Floster's graduation from the school.

A history of Schofield Normal and Industrial School

Founded in 1871 by Martha Schofield, a Pennsylvania Quaker, this Aiken school for freed slaves remained a center of education for black South Carolinians for more than seventy years. The school's initial financial support came from Schofield, the John F. Slater Fund, and other Quakers from Pennsylvania. Unfortunately, these contributions proved to be inadequate, and the financial burden fell entirely to Schofield, who used her personal fortune to sustain the school until she resigned in 1912. The school operated in the original Freedman's Bureau school building until 1882, when a new building was constructed. The school began as a day school, and from its beginning the goal was to prepare teachers who were desperately needed in the state's rural black schools. As with most freedmen's schools, the curriculum was a simplified version of the classical course of study.

Schofield was also the site for a summer Colored Teachers' Institute where teaching methods, teacher qualifications, and community-school relations were discussed. With more than twenty years of training teachers, the state board of education recognized the school's success by granting it university status in 1908, and later graduates were automatically licensed to teach without taking county or state examinations. Initially vocal in their animosity toward the school and its students, the white community eventually came to praise the students for their dependability and skills. The school joined the Aiken school system in 1953 as a public high school for blacks. Since integration in the 1960s, Schofield has served Aiken County as a public middle school, and the bell tower from the original building still sat on the Sumter Street campus in the early twenty-first century.

Source: https://www.scencyclopedia.org/sce/entries/schofield-normal-and-industrial-school/

The Original Bell Tower of Schofield Normal and Industrial School

The remainder of the original school is the bell tower, which is at the entrance of the school grounds of Schofield Middle School in Aiken, South Carolina.

Source: https://www.postandcourier.com/aikenstandard/education/aiken-county-students-receive-martha-schofield-scholarships/article

The Original Schofield Normal and Industrial School Staff

The staff of the original Schofield Normal and Industrial School. Martha Schofield, far right, helped construct the school in Aiken where Schofield Middle School is now located.

Source: https://www.postandcourier.com/aikenstandard/education/aiken-county-students-receive-martha-schofield-scholarships/article

Wharton Hall-Early Men's Dormitory at Schofield Normal and Industrial School

Verlenden Hall-Women's Dormitory at Schofield Normal and Industrial School

Contributor: Courtesy of Martha Schofield High School Rams Assoication

Schofield Normal and Industrial School faculty & students
Source: Courtesy of Martha Schofield High School Rams Alumni
Association

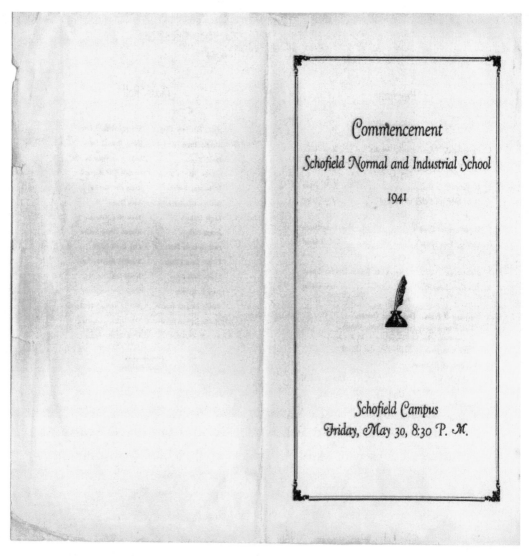

Schofield Normal and Industrial School Commencement Program Front Page

The commencement took place on Friday May 30th, 1941 at 8:30 PM

Source: Martha Schofield High School Rams Alumni Association

Program

1. Processional, "Priests' March, 'Athalia'" .... *Mendelssohn*
2. "Fairest Lord Jesus" .... *Wesley and Mason*
   Choir
3. Invocation .... Rev. M. M. Peace
4. "Dear Lord and Father of Mankind" .... *Fred Maker*
   Choir
5. Commencement Speaker .... Miss Joyce Mason
6. "Lift Up Your Heads" .... *E. L. Ashford*
   Choir
7. Address .... Rev. C. H. Brown, Benedict College
8. "On Great Lone Hills" .... *Jean Sibelius*
   Quartette
9. Awarding of Prizes: Declamation Contest.
   First Prize given by Friendship Baptist Church.
   Second Prize given by Cumberland A. M. E. Church
   Third Prize given by Wesley Methodist Church
10. Awarding of Diplomas
11. Evening Prayer .... *Charles Gabriel*
    Choir
12. Benediction
13. Recessional

Class Roll

Hattie Elizabeth Allen	Gilbert Nathaniel Jones
Alzenia Alston	Marion Howard Jones
Aaron Busch	*Beatrice Gardinia Kenner
Dorothy Beatrice Busch	*Fannie Louise Marshall
Wilhelmina Butler	Maxie Mae Marshall
Beatrice Cunningham	*Joyce Mason
Emily Dicks	Annie Mae Nicholson
Joseph Dicks	Mildred Elease Nobles
Cartrell Louis Draft	King David Odom
Floster Leon Ellison	Lubertha Dorothy Scott
Noesie Belle Gyles	*Jewell Edith Smith
*Jesse E. Halmon	*Wilber Alvin Strother
Estella Luvenia Jackson	Warren Harding Thompson
*Marion Luvenia Johnson	Charles Booker Walker
Ruth Mae Johnson	Ellen Alberta Young

*Honor Students

Schofield Normal and Industrial School Commencement Program outline and class roll

The class roll list Floster Leon Ellison as a graduate. His cousin, Warren Harding Thompson, son of Oscar J. & Lessie Felder Thompson, is listed.

Source: Martha Schofield High School Rams Alumni Association

APPENDIX XV– FLOSTER L. ELLISON, JR. COLLEGE GRADUATION RECORDS & EXPERIENCE

During the 1950s, Floster began to progressively transform his life. He received his bachelor's degree from Benedict College in 1954 and pursued graduate studies at Clark Atlanta University a few years later and earned a master's degree in social work in 1960. While at Clark Atlanta, on April 17, 1957, Floster participated in a town meeting titled "How Can Students Make the World Better?" with faculty and fellow students and wrote his thesis titled, *"A Study of the Social Service Convalescent Program at Northville State Hospital, and Patients' Reaction to the Program"*.

This section includes:

1. The Atlanta University Bulletin (Newsletter), S. III No. 103: July 1958 and The Atlanta University Bulletin (Catalogue), S. III No. 106;1958-1959; Announcements 1959-1960.
2. Floster L. Ellison, Jr. master's thesis title page and acknowledgements
3. Floster L. Ellison Jr., college picture

> TOWN MEETING: April 17 — Dr. Howard Zinn, Spelman College, Mrs. Jamye Williams, Morris Brown College, Miss Christine Johnson, Clark College, Floster L. Ellison, Atlanta University, James Shaw, Morehouse College. "How Can Students Make the World Better?"

The Atlanta University Bulletin (Newsletter), S. III No. 103: July 1958

While attending Clark Atlanta University, on April 17, 1957, Floster participated in a town meeting titled "How Can Students Make the World Better?"

> ELLISON, FLOSTER LEON ....Columbia, S. C.
>   A.B., Benedict College, 1954.

The Atlanta University Bulletin (Catalogue), S. III No. 106;1958–1959; Announcements 1959–1960

Floster L. Ellison earned his Bachelor of Arts degree from Benedict College in 1954

Sources: http://hdl.handle.net/20.500.12322/fa:002

A STUDY OF THE SOCIAL SERVICE CONVALESCENT PROGRAM
AT NORTHVILLE STATE HOSPITAL, AND THE
PATIENTS' REACTION TO THE PROGRAM

A THESIS
SUBMITTED TO THE FACULTY OF ATLANTA UNIVERSITY
IN PARTIAL FULFILLMENT OF THE REQUIREMENTS FOR
THE DEGREE OF MASTER OF SOCIAL WORK

BY
FLOSTER LEON ELLISON, JR.

SCHOOL OF SOCIAL WORK

ATLANTA, GEORGIA
JUNE 1959

Master Thesis Title Page

Source: http://hdl.handle.net/20.500.12322/cau.td:1959_ellison_jr_floster_1

ACKNOWLEDGMENTS

Gratitude for encouragement and helpful assistance
in the writing of this thesis is expressed to Mr. Kenneth
Ives, Research Coordinator, Dr. G. F. Hewman, Acting Director of the Out-Patient Department, and other members
of the staff of Northville State Hospital, for their assistance and cooperation in offering helpful suggestions
and guidance during the initial stages of the study; to
Mr. Warren H. Moore, Atlanta University School of Social
Work for his patience and guidance throughout the writing
of this thesis; and to my wife, Mrs. Alice Marie Ellison
and sons for their prayers, interest and moral support.

Master's Thesis acknowledgements

Source: http://hdl.handle.net/20.500.12322/cau.td:1959_ellison_jr_floster_

Floster L. Ellison, Jr., graduation picture

Date unknown

APPENDIX XVI–FLOSTER L. ELLISON, JR. WORLD WAR II SERVICE

On February 7, 1942, the navy announced that African Americans would be enlisted in general and messman service beginning on June 1, 1942. The following year, on February 1, 1943, roughly 20,000 African American sailors were messman. A few months later, on May 15, 1943, Floster enlisted in the navy and acquired the skill of barbering, which became a lifelong passion.

This section includes:

1. An image of Floster L. Ellison, Jr., World War II draft registration card
2. An image of Floster L Ellison, Jr. World War II Pennsylvania World War II Veteran application file
3. A picture of Floster L. Ellison, Jr. in Navy uniform with his wife, Alice Marie Ellison

Image of Floster L. Ellison, Jr., World War II draft registration card

Source: Ancestry.com. U.S., World War II Draft Cards Young Men, 1940-1947

Form No. 1 ～～—10

COMMONWEALTH OF PENNSYLVANIA
WORLD WAR II VETERANS' COMPENSATION BUREAU

APPLICATION FOR WORLD WAR II COMPENSATION—TO BE USED BY HONORABLY DISCHARGED VETERAN OR PERSON STILL IN SERVICE

IMPORTANT—Before Filling Out This Form Study it Carefully.
Read and Follow Instructions—Print Plainly in Ink or Use Typewriter. DO NOT Use Pencil—All Signatures Must Be in Ink.

Applicant Must Not Write In Space Below

MAY 3 1950
Date Application Was Received

1—Name of Applicant.

Ellison   Floster   Leon Jr.
Last   First   Middle or Initial

Batch Control Number

16695

2—Address to Which CHECK and MAIL is to be Sent.   38

2312 Starks St. Apt. 3   Columbia   Richland   S.C.
House No. St. R. D. P. O. Box   City or Town   County   State

Active Domestic Service
Months 31 $ 310
Days
Amount Due $ 310

3—Date and Place of Birth.

10   10   22   Aiken   Aiken   S.C.
Month   Day   Year   City or Town   County   State

Active Foreign Service
Months $
Days $
Amount Due $

4—Name Under Which Applicant Served In World War II.

Ellison   Floster   Leon Jr.
Last   First   Middle or Initial

Total Amt. Due $ 310

5—Date of Beginning and Date of Ending of Each Period of Service Between December 7, 1941 and March 2, 1946 (Both Dates Inclusive) During Which Applicant Was In DOMESTIC SERVICE.

nov.
5-15-43   31-4   dec. 12-17-45

Date of Beginning   Date of Ending

Audited By

Service Computed By   Boyle

Amounts Extended By   Mallon

6—Date of Beginning and Date of Ending of Each Period of Service Between December 7, 1941 and March 2, 1946 (Both Dates Inclusive) During Which Applicant Was In FOREIGN SERVICE.

Approved For Payment
MAY 11 1950

Date
For A. G.   Mallon

Date of Beginning   Date of Ending

For Aud. G.

7—Date and Place Applicant Entered Active Service.

5   15   43   Philadelphia, Pa.
Month Day   Year   Place

For S. T.   Robert

Application Disapproved

By

8—Service or Serial Numbers Assigned To Applicant.

Service No's.

Serial No's.   817-65-68

9—Date and Place Where Applicant Was Separated From Active Service.

12   17   45   New Orleans, La.
Month   Day   Year   Place

10—Is Applicant Now Serving In Armed Forces On Active Duty?   Yes _____   No ✓
If Answer is YES—Be Sure To Have Certificate Executed And Filed With Application—See Instruction Sheet.

11—Mark "X" Above Name To Indicate Sex And Branch of Service.

X   X
Male   Female   Army   Navy   Marine Corps   Coast Guard   Other—Describe

12—Applicant's Residence At Time of Entry Into Active Service.

1579   Brown   Philadelphia   Phila.   Pa.
House No.   Street   R. D.   P. O. Box   City or Town   County   State

13—Applicant Was Registered Under Selective Service As Follows.

9   Philadelphia   Phila.   Pa.
Draft Board No.   City or Town   County   State

Image of Floster L Ellison, Jr. World War II Pennsylvania World War II Veteran application file

Source: Ancestry.com. Pennsylvania, U.S., Veteran Compensation Application Files, WWII, 1950–1966

Floster L. Ellison, Jr. in Navy uniform with his wife, Alice Marie Ellison

Date Unknown

APPENDIX XVII–THE PALMETTO STATE
BARBER ASSOCIATION

Inspired by the activism of the Civil Rights Movement, on July 18, 1960, Floster L. Ellison, Jr., and Luther Lilliewood, along with several others, founded the Palmetto State Barbers Association. The founding purpose was to "encourage the practice of barbering as a profession and to promote ethical principles and practices therein; to increase the usefulness of the profession to the public and to create a better understanding and a more meaningful relationship among the barbers of South Carolina." The association's charge was given by Floster with these encouraging words: "Barber, one who shaves and trims the beard and cuts the air. The trade of barbering is one of great antiquity." The association envisioned itself as a collaborative entity, unifying licensed professional African American barbers to promote the values of professionalism, integrity, education, and service; it would become a civic organization whose members would serve the community in which they lived and work. Shortly after, Floster's term ended in 1970, the association successfully lobbied the State Board of Barber Examiners for African American representation on the board, and members ran for political office in their respective communities.

This section includes:

1. An image of the Palmetto Barber Association Certificate of Incorporation.
2. A picture of Willie Anderson-Member of the Palmetto State Barber Association and possessor of the original Palmetto Barber Association Certificate of Incorporation
3. "Vaugh Running for Commission" newspaper article
4. "Rainey Issue Statement" newspaper article
5. "Negro Barbers Charge Discrimination In S.C." newspaper article
6. "Named to Board" newspaper article
7. "New Law on Barber Examiner Challenged" newspaper article
8. A picture of Jessie Mae Manning-The first African American female licensed barber in Cherokee County and member of the Palmetto State Barber Association

The R. L. Bryan Company, Columbia, S. C.

5665

The State of South Carolina | CERTIFICATE OF INCORPORATION
EXECUTIVE DEPARTMENT | BY THE SECRETARY OF STATE

WHEREAS,

F. L. ELLISON, JR., and LUTHER LILLIEWOOD

both of

Columbia, S. C.

DISSOLVED BY FORFEITURE

DATE MAR 17 1975

FAILURE

two or more of the officers or agents appointed to supervise or manage the affairs of

PALMETTO BARBERS ASSOCIATION
(Columbia, S. C.)

which has been duly and regularly organized, did on the 18th day of

July , A.D. 1960 , file with the Secretary of State a written declaration setting forth:

That, at a meeting of the aforesaid organization held pursuant to the by-laws or regulations of the said organization, they were authorized and directed to apply for incorporation.

That, the said organization holds, or desires to hold, property in common for Religious, Educational, Social, Fraternal, Charitable or other eleemosynary purpose, or any two or more of said purposes, and is not organized for the purpose of profit or gain to the members, otherwise than is above stated, nor for the insurance of life, health, accident or property; and that three days' notice in the The State , a newspaper published in the County of Richland , has been given that the aforesaid Declaration would be filed.

And Whereas, Said Declarants and Petitioners further declared and affirmed:

FIRST: Their names and residences are as above given.

SECOND: The name of the proposed Corporation is PALMETTO BARBERS ASSOCIATION

THIRD: The place at which it proposes to have its headquarters or be located is COLUMBIA, S. C.

FOURTH: The purpose of the said proposed Corporation is to encourage the practice of barbering as a profession and to promote ethical principles and practices therein; to increase the usefulness of the profession to the public and to create a better understanding and a more meaningful relationship among the barbers of South Carolina.

FIFTH: The names and residences of all Managers, Trustees, Directors or other officers are as follows:

F. L. Ellison, Jr.	Columbia, S. C.	President
Luther Lilliewood	Columbia, S. C.	Vice-President
Frank V. Davis	Columbia, S. C.	Secretary
F. D. Stephens	Columbia, S. C.	Treasurer
George E. Patterson	Columbia, S. C.	Director
Theodore Perrin	Columbia, S. C.	Director
Uzell Hoefer	Columbia, S. C.	Director
Robert Bossard	Columbia, S. C.	Director

SIXTH: That they desire to be incorporated: In perpetuity.

Now, Therefore, I, O. FRANK THORNTON, Secretary of State, by virtue of the authority in me vested, by Chapter 12, Title 12, Code of 1952, and Acts amendatory thereto, do hereby declare the said organization to be a body politic and corporate, with all the rights, powers, privileges and immunities, and subject to all the limitations and liabilities, conferred by said Chapter 12, Title 12, Code of 1952, and Acts amendatory thereto.

GIVEN under my hand and the seal of the State, at Columbia, this 18th day of July in the year of our Lord one thousand nine hundred and 60 and in the one hundred and 85th year of the Independence of the United States of America.

O. FRANK THORNTON,
Secretary of State.

Palmetto Barbers Association Certificate of Incorporation

The Palmetto Barbers Association was chartered on July 18th, 1960. Floster L. Ellison, Jr. and Luther Lilliewood filed the certificated of incorporation at the South Carolina Secretary of State office.

Source: South Carolina Department of Archives and History

Mr. Willie Anderson

Member of the Palmetto State Barber Association and possessor of the original Palmetto Barbers Association Certificate of Incorporation.

Vaughn Running For Commission

By BOB CRAFT
ITEM Staff Writer

Sidney Vaughn

Sidney Vaughn is seeking a post on the Sumter County Commission, which has four seats up for election this year.

"I have lived with, worked with and served the people of Sumter and Sumter County all my life; and I feel that I can best represent the county," Vaughn said in making his statement of candidacy.

"The county needs more industry to create jobs for the many unemployed citizens in and around Sumter and Sumter County. As a member of the county commission, I will work hard to bring more industry into the county. More industry means more taxes, better paid teachers and quality education," Vaughn said.

In his try for office, Vaughn promised a "clean and humble campaign" and "due to my experience from working in plants and different industries, I will never impose on working voters to pass out literature when they are entering the plant for work or coming out after a long tiresome day of running

Continued on Page 2A

machines. I know they are tired and hungry and only wish to get home," said Vaughn.

He said instead, he will have campaign meetings to discuss county political affairs.

A licensed barber for 24 years, Vaughn is affiliated with the Palmetto State Barber's Association where he has served two consecutive terms as president. Also with the professional organization, he has served on the Steering, Nominating and Public Relations Committees.

In 1974, Vaughn was named 'Barber of the Year" by the Palmetto State Barber's Association.

He has been; first vice-president of the Sumter and Sumter County NAACP for the past eight years and has sat on a citizen's committee which drew up the first guidelines for poverty programs in Sumter County.

Vaughn is a past vice-president of the Sumter High Booster Club, a past member of the lay board of visitors for School District 17 and from 1970 to 1972, worked as an ombudsman for Sumter High School.

He attends St. Luke AME Church where he serves on the Steward Board. Vaughn is a past member of the Trustee board, which he served on for 16 years.

He is married to the former Lillie Holloman and they have two sons.

Miles Entering . . .

Continued From Page 1A

Society Division Board, the Executive Committee, and S.C. Educational Funds Crusade Regional Director for Sumter, Lee, Clarendon and Kershaw Counties; Radio and Television Commission of the S.C. Baptist

"Vaugh Running for Commission", The Item, March 22, 1976

Sidney Vaugh was a licensed barber for 24 years and served two consecutive terms as President of the Palmetto State Barbers Association. He ran for a seat on the Sumter County Commission.

Source: https://www.newspapers.com/clip/69030779/palmetto-state-barbers/

Harvey F. Rainey

Rainey Issues Statement

Harvey F. Rainey has issued a statement in support of his candidacy for the office of Councilman from Ward 4.

Mr. Rainey's statement is as follows:

"I am offering myself as a candidate for the City Council in Ward 4.

"I am a resident of the City of Gaffney and reside at Poplar Springs Drive. I am married to the former Laurichard Smith and we have two children, Ramona 17 and Harvey, III 15. I am a member of A. M. E. Zion Church serving on the Steward Board, serving as the Pastor's Steward. I am a member of the Palmetto Barber's Association and am president of the Spartanburg, Gaffney Chapter. I am a member of the Board of Directors for the Boys' Club in Cherokee County. I am also a Mason.

"It is my desire to become a part of the City Council, because I am interested in the progress of Gaffney and the well being of all residents.

"If elected, I will support any efforts, plans or endeavors within reason that will help to up-grade Gaffney or benefit the people therein.

(Continued on Page 2)

From Page One

"I will oppose any plans, motions or ventures that I feel will be detrimental or degrading to our city.

"If elected, I will also speak against any abuse or misrepresentation that might disqualify or lower the standards of the Council, the Government and the City of Gaffney.

"Since residing in Gaffney I have taken a close look at our city streets and public buildings and have noticed that some are in need of repair.

"These and many more improvements can be made with a City Council of interested, cooperative and dedicated men. I feel the present City Council consists of men with these characteristics, and if elected I will work cooperatively with the other Aldermen in order to maintain these characteristics and help to continue the progress already displayed by them.

"If elected, I feel that I will be an asset to the City Council and the city of Gaffney, because I can best serve the people of Gaffney if placed in a position were my ideas, desires, and interests for this great city can best be put into action.

"If elected to the seat of Alderman for Ward 4; I am sure that along with the other five Alderman we can continue to make Gaffney a pleasant, safe and progressive city in which to live."

"Rainey Issues Statement", The Gaffney Ledger, December 24, 1971

Harvey F. Rainey was licensed barber and member of the Palmetto Barber's Assoication and president of the Spartanburg Gaffney Chapter who ran for Gaffney City Council Ward 4.

Source: https://www.newspapers.com/clip/64165310/palmetto-barbers-association-harvey/

Negro Barbers Charge Discrimination In S. C.

By THE ASSOCIATED PRESS

South Carolina's Negro barbers claim the state is discriminating against them because no Negroes are members of the state Board of Barber Examiners.

Sidney Vaughn of Sumter, president of the Palmetto Barbers Association, which represents 1,300 black barbers, charged yesterday that a white barber cannot tell if a Negro has received a "grade A haircut."

Until the late 1950's, Vaughn said, barbers' textbooks did not even teach students how to cut Negroes' hair because "white men wrote the books."

Thus, Vaughn continued, present board members aren't qualified to examine prospective Negro barbers.

At a recent convention, the Palmetto Barbers Association passed a resolution urging Gov. Robert McNair to allow the state's registered barbers to elect the three members of the examing board.

"We could elect at least one black representative" if this step were taken, Vaughn asserted. He said that more than 40 percent of the barbers in South Carolina are black.

The members of the examining body are currently appointed by the governor for three-year terms.

A spokesman for Gov. McNair told The State newspaper yesterday that the black barbers' resolution had not yet reached the governor. But the governor "would be happy to receive recommendations from any interested group" about upcoming appointments to the board, the spokesman added.

There is no opening on the board until next June.

> If we do well, I predict that all the laws will be repealed in two years. If we botch the job, it will set us back a decade.
> —*Dr. Robert Hall, president of the Association for the Study of Abortion, commenting on New York's new abortion law, most liberal in the nation.*

Police Reports

City detectives are investigating the grand larceny of two tape players which occurred during the 24-hour period ending at 11 p.m. Monday.

car, and the tape player and nine tapes were removed.

The tape player was valued at $110 and the tapes were valued at a total of $45.

A case of malicious mischief

"Negro Barbers Charge Discrimination In S.C.", The Item, July 21, 1970

In this artilce, the Palmetto State Barber Assoication claimed that South Carolina are discriminating against them because no Negroes were members of the state Board of Barber Examiners.

Source: https://www.newspapers.com/clip/64137890/palmetto-barbers-association-fl-ellison/

Named to Board

Harvey F. Rainey, Gaffney barber, has been named as a member of the State Board of Barber Examiners by Gov. John C. West. Rainey was named to a four-year term along with Robert R. Martin of Spartanburg.

"Named to Board", The Gaffney Ledger, June 30, 1972

In this article, Harvey F. Rainiey, member of the Palmetto Barber Assoication, was named as a member of the South Carolina State Board of Barber Examiners by Gov. John C. West.

Source: https://www.newspapers.com/clip/64165422/palmetto-barbers-association-harvey

New Law On Barber Examiners Challenged

COLUMBIA (AP)-A new law reconstituting membership on the South Carolina State Board of Barber Examiners has been challenged in a suit filed in the Richland County Court of Common Pleas.

Columbia barber Kenneth S. Watts asks that the law be declared unconstitutional because of the method of appointing members to the board.

The new law provides that the board be enlarged from three to five members, with three to be appointed by the governor upon the recommendation of the Executive Board of the Associated Master Barbers of South Carolina and the other two members appointed by the governor on recommendation of the Executive Committee of the Palmetto State Barbers Association.

Under the old law, the governor appointed the three members without the recomendation of any group.

Watts contends neither the predominantly white Associated Master Barbers nor the predominantly black Palmetto Barbers Association speaks for a majority of the 3,300 barbers in the state.

He said in a statement that division of the board along racial lines contravenes the due process and equal protection clauses of the state and federal constitutions.

Watts also criticized a provision of the new law increasing the annual registration fee for barber shops from $7.50 to $25.

"In these days of inflation and long hair, which means fewer haircuts, the average barber is caught in the squeeze," said Watts.

Vote At Charleston May Be Thrown Out

COLUMBIA (AP)-The State Board of Canvassers took under advisement Tuesday a request to throw out the results of a June 8 Democratic primary in which veteran Charleston Mayor J. Palmer Gaillard was declared renominated.

Attorneys for Charleston law-

ic municipal primary. Ackerman's attorneys argued that persons who voted in both were not legally entitled to do so.

They cited a recent advisory opinion of State Atty. Gen. Daniel R. McLeod as backing up their contention.

"New Law on Barber Examiner Challenged", The Times and Democrat, July 8th, 1971

In this article, Columbia barber Kenneth S. Watts filed a lawsuit that challenged the law that enlargd the South Carolina State Board of Barber examiners from three to five. Watts contended neither the predominantly white associated Masters Barbers nor the predominatly black Palmetto Barbers Association speaks for a majority of the 3,300 barbers in the state.

Source: https://www.newspapers.com/clip/64139858/palmetto-barbers-association-fl/

Jessie Mae Manning

Jessie Mae Manning is a graduate of Granard High School Class of 1956. She attended Denmark Area Trade School where she majored in barbering and attended Limestone College. She became the first African American female barber in Cherokee County. Jessie Mae joined the Palmetto Barber Association and served as assistant secretary of Spartanburg/Gaffney Chapter No.6 of the Association. An active community activitst involved in many civic organizations, she served as the first African American female president of the Chreokee County Branch of the NAACP, and ran for Gaffney City Council District No.2 & Cherokee County School Board. Jessie Mae was inducted into the Cherokee County NAACP Hall of Fame in 1998.

Contributor: Courtesey of Nick Drayton, grandson of Jessie Mae Manning

P.S-The photo on the right is Jessie Mae cutting a gentlemen's hair in the chair

APPENDIX XVIII–SOUTH CAROLINA STATE BOARD OF BARBER EXAMINERS MINUTES

Floster L. Ellison, Jr. was elected as the association's first president and served until 1970. During his early tenure, the association focused on cracking down on unlicensed barbers and lobbied the state government for African American representation on the State Board of Barber Examiners. On September 11, 1963, Floster spoke before the board about the prospect of hiring an African American inspector.

The board was so impressed with Floster's eloquence based on his profound knowledge, they wanted to hire him as an inspector on the spot. He was interested in the position but wanted to confer with the association to discuss the matter before accepting the position. On October 4, 1963, Floster was hired as the first African American barber inspector in the state of South Carolina, with a salary of $17.50 per day, plus mileage and expenses. He primarily inspected African American-owned barbershops and occasionally White-owned barbershops. It was Floster's mission during his inspections to ensure that barbers were professionally capable and qualified to do their jobs according to the law and adhere to professional standards.

This section includes:

1. A excerpt of September 11th, 1963 South Carolina State Board of Barber Examiners minutes.
2. A excerpt of October 9th, 1963 minutes South Carolina State Board of Barber Examiners minutes.
3. "Chief Barber Inspector Talks to Association" newspaper article

A number of colored barbers from the Columbia Barber Association met with the Board
in regard to putting on a colored Inspector. Mr. Floster L. Ellison was spokesman for
the group.

Mr. Ellison: We are members of the Columbia Barber Association, which is a Negro
Oranginzation, primarily for the betterment of barber shops and for customers of these
shops. About a month ago we went down and talked to the Governor in regard to getting
some representation with the Board. He was very receptive of us. I was told by Mr.
George Patterson that there might be a chance of getting an Inspector. Our hope at
this time is to support the Barber Board. We don't have to account to any one person.
We are not dictated to by any outside organization or group. There are many things that
we could do that you might not be able to do. Our hope is to work with you and support
you. We are not trying to dictate. We are with every effort the Board puts forth.
We have been able to get barbers in our organization that are most interested in the
barber profession. We have many violators and we think that we can be a help to the
Board in locating these violators. That is our reason for asking to meet with you today.

Mr. Long: First, I knew of this Ellison is when the Governor called me in on it. As I
have said before, we would like to put on two or three Inspectors. I intimated to the
Governor that we might put on one Inepsector for one day a week. The Board has talked
to the Governor about this. I, personally will have to lean on you people for the right
kind of man to employ as Inspector.

Mr. Merritt: Of course the Barber Board's records are open for inspection. The Board
feels that we might have a man one day a week at this time. It is difficult for the
Inspectors to find any violators without your help.

Mr. Lane: Actually, we can't catch all the violators. You might be able to locate
them much better than we can. When the Inspectors go into a section they are very
easily spotted and it is hard to catch anyone barbering. We have violators that barber
at night and even on Sunday. We might have to ask the Inspector to work some on
Sunday to catch these violators.

Excerpt of September 11th, 1963 South Carolina State Board of Barber Examiners

On September 11, 1963, Floster spoke before the board about the prospect of hiring an African
American inspector. (Floster is known as **Mr. Ellison** in the minutes)

Mr. Ellison: We have discussed this Pro and Con and we agree with you. There are many violators. We know we have some Sunday morning violators.

Mr. Merritt: We had an example of this in Sumter. Several back yard violators were caught. They were convicted. Two of them have appealed and case is still pending.

Mr. Ellison: Of course with this kind of person, cutting hair in house or back yard, a colored Inspector might be able to get in and catch them quicker. An incompetent person like these violators can destroy our progess or good will that we can build up. We are with the Board and want to help anyway we can.

Mr. Long: At this time I think that we can put on a man one day a week. Do you have any man in mind?

Mr. Ellison: We have approximately 60 members. We feel that out of this number we should be able to recommend a person that we would not be ashamed of and you would not be ashamed to put him to work with the Board. If he leaves his shop all day on Saturday, he wouldn't have very much. That is the day we have the most business. Person employed must be a capable man. We can give you two or three names on Monday and let you decide.

Mr. Long: What about you?

Mr. Ellison: If I said I would accept it, the group would go along with it. I would like to discuss it with them. I am President. I'd like to discuss it with them and if some other responsible person would accept, I'd go along with them.

Mr. Lane: This will be the making or breaking of the work. Just because you are President, I don't think you should be by passed. Sometimes a capable man is by passed in this way.

Mr. Ellison: I would be able to accept and do the work. My work would not interfer with working as an Inspector. However, I would still like to call a meeting and discuss it.

Mr. Sellers: I feel that you can pay your way by catching the violators that we haven't been able to catch. There are a lot of them that are getting by without complying with the law.

Excerpt of September 11th, 1963 South Carolina State Board of Barber Examiners (con't)

Mr. Lane: This is the thinking of this Board. The Inspector would almost have to be

a resident of this City. The main towns are Charleston, Greenville and Columbia. We

might ask you to check some other place.

Mr. Sellers: You would be sent where you are needed.

Mr. Long: Ellison, who ever takes this job, we will pay them $17.50 a day, allow 8 cents

mileage and something for meals. We want ask you to do anymore than the other Inspectors.

The Board agreed to go along with this group and hire the person they recommend.

Mr. Long: Ellison, I think you made a wonderful statement to the Board. I appreciated

what you said. Mr. Lane and Mr. Sellers also expressed their appreciation of the interest

shown.

Mr. Long: When a man is recommended, I will call the other members of this Board and

confirm their approval and the man will be put to work. I will go with him on the first,

inspection, if this is agreeable with you all. The Board agreed to this.
                    Assistant
Letter read from the Attorney General in regard to Student permits and place on file

Excerpt of September 11th, 1963 South Carolina State Board of Barber Examiners (con't)

As per September minutes, Mr. Long contacted the other Board Members and F. L. Ellison,

was employed as of October 4, 1963 as colored Inspector for part time work. Salary

$17.50 per day, mileage and expense. Mr. Long worked with him October 4th. His

report and suggestions were checked by the Board.

Excertpt of October 9th, 1963 minutes South Carolina State Board of Barber Examiners minutes

On October 4, 1963, Floster was hired as the first African American barber inspector in the state of South Carolina, with a salary of $17.50 per day, plus mileage and expenses

Chief Barber Inspector Talks To Association

F. L. Ellison, inspector for the State Board of Barber Examiners and president of the state Palmetto Barbers Association, urged members of the Master Barbers Association to be men of honor, character and dignity at a meeting of the organization held recently.

Ellison said that unless the barbers meet present - day challenges and organize their efforts, the cause of barbering will suffer for lack of interest among young people wh would go into the profession.

Thomas Hayes, instructor in barbering, and the graduating class of the South Carolina Area Trade School in Denmark attended the meeting.

W. L. (Bill) Davis, president of the local association, presided at the meeting.

Chief Barber Inspector Talks To Association, Times and Democrat, March 25, 1965

In this artilce, Floster L. Ellison, Sr., inspector for the State Board of Barber Examinerrs and President of the state Palmetto Barbers Association spoke during a meeting with the Master Barbers Association, an organization comprised of predominantly White barbers.

Source: https://www.newspapers.com/clip/64138086/fl-ellison-palmetto-barber-association/

APPENDIX XX– Palmetto State Hospital

In conjunction with his flourishing barbering career, Floster L. Ellison, Jr. was determined to suc-ceed in the field of social work. In the early 1960s, he was employed as a case worker at Palmetto State Hospital, which was a mental health facility for African American patients operated by the South Carolina Department of Mental Health. In the summer of 1965, Floster was promoted to chief of social services of the hospital Division of Social Services. Floster, along with his nephew who worked under him, Otis Corbitt, successfully increased the number of African American employees at the hospital, several of whom were Benedict College graduates, and even recruited an employee from Salley, Francis Williams, a graduate from Tuskegee University.

This section includes::

1. The Variety Newsletter, Vol. 13, No.10, November 1965 that documents Floster work at Palmetto State Hospital

PALMETTO STATE HOSPITAL

| Sol B. McLendon, M. D. | Leon M. Elam |
| Director of Professional Services and Medical Director | Associate Editor |

SOCIAL SERVICE

Mr. F. L. Ellison, Chief
Mrs. Alice Hurley, Reporter

The Social Service Department at Palmetto State Hospital has been growing by leaps and bounds, recently. If you and your department are feeling our growing pains, please be patient and work with us.

Since June, we have had six new workers to join our staff. We introduced most of them to you in the September 17 issue of the Weekly Bulletin, but we wish to do so, again, since we have continued to grow since that time.

By now, Receiving Building should be familiar with Miss Roberta Hampton who joined the staff in June. She is from Camden and worked last year in the Darlington Public School System. Miss Hampton is a graduate of Johnson C. Smith University in Charlotte, N. C. She will cover all social services and staffings related to the admissions service.

Mr. Augustus Rodgers began working in July. He is a recent graduate of Benedict College and also recently became a new father. He, along with Mr. McIlwain, will be assigned our court cases and Shand Building, and may be seen on any ward.

Mr. William J. McIlwain, our newest member, is a native Columbian and a recent graduate of Benedict. He is a French major and was cited in Who's Who in Colleges and Universities in the U. S. and Canada, January, 1964. In addition to becoming acclimated to his new job, Mr. McIlwain will be assisting Mr. Rodgers in traveling on court cases and will be the worker for Building 6. He is also single, girls!

Miss Selena Felder who came to us in August is probably well known by now. In addition to being the fashion-plate of the department, she will be working with the patients and staff of Building 15, 7, 4 and 16 (Women). Miss Felder is a May, 1965 graduate of Benedict College

The Rehab Department is fortunate to have Miss Francis Williams to replace Mr. Otis Corbitt who is now away in school. She is a Tuskegee Institute Alumnus and hails from the Sally-Springfield area. Miss Williams joined us in September.

Buildings 3, 12, 5 and 16 (men) will be covered by Mrs. Evelyn Hill who also joined us in September. She is a Benedict Alumnus and taught last year in the Columbia Public Schools.

Our old personnel are making changes, also. Mr. Thomas Davis, Mr. Willie Josey and Mrs. Alice Hurley have recently been transferred to Building 13 to work with the new HIP Project. We hope to get the entire hospital interested in this project because we feel that understanding promotes acceptance and cooperation.

Mrs. Means who is also familiar to us all, will continue to work with Buildings 10, 1-B, 1-C, 11 and has been newly assigned to Davis Building.

Mrs. Mary M. Wilson, whom we have known for a long time and has recently come back to us from Pineland, is our desk worker. She will also be working with Buildings 2, 8 and 14.

Mr. Ellison who was recently promoted this past summer from Acting Chief to Chief of Social Service, is still running the show. To him goes the credit for recruiting our new staff members. He continues to be very active in hospital and community activities. In particular, we wish to commend his services with the Waverly Social Club which has been a guiding light for many ex-patients and patients who are on their way out of the hospital.

Our workers will be making routinely scheduled visits to your buildings but we encourage you to call on us whenever the need arises at extension 784 or 785. Mrs. Wilson will be happy to relay your message to the appropriate worker.

****

The Variety Newsletter, Vol. 13, No.10, November 1965

In this article, it states that "Mr. Ellison who was recently promoted this past summer from Acting Chief to Chief of Social Service, is still running the show. To him goes the credit for recruting our new staff mmebers. He continues to be very active in hospital and community activities"

Source: The South Carolina State Library

APPENDIX XIX–Crafts Farrow State Hopsital

The Palmetto State Hospital drew the ire of the Richland County Citizens Committee. The committee leader, Modjeska Simkins, who was an important leader in public health reform during the Civil Rights Movement, highlighted the deplorable conditions of the hospital. The committee's grievances undergirded the reasoning of the Civil Rights of Act of 1964 that required the desegregation of public facilities and provision of equitable accommodations. In 1965, the South Carolina Department of Mental Health integrated, and the former Palmetto Hospital was renamed Crafts-Farrow State Hospital. This resulted in substantial improvements within the hospital that included maintenance upgrades and reform in mental health services. Floster L. Ellison, Jr. became the first director of Social Services at Crafts-Farrow and served in that capacity for the next twenty years.

This section includes:

1. A letter of The Richland County Citizens Committee, Inc. written by Modjeska Simkins.
2. A picture of Modjeska Simkins
3. Images of the History of Crafts-Farrow State Hospital
4. The Variety Newsletter, Vol. 15, Nos.10-11, October-November 1967

The Richland County Citizens Committee, Inc.

ORGANIZED IN 1944 • CHARTERED IN 1956
1808 WASHINGTON STREET • AL 2-9573
COLUMBIA, SOUTH CAROLINA

January 25, 1965

To the Honorable Members of the
96th General Assembly

Sirs:

    The enclosed copy adressed to the Honorable Donald S. Russel, Governor, and presented to him by our committee on December 7, outlines among other things the deplorable conditions at the Palmetto State Hospital (Negro asylum). This set-up was diabolically segregated, renamed, and absolutely divorced by legislative act inspired by and condoned by the Mental Health Commission, while the Bull Street facility was upgraded, updated, and gloriously certified with the full-blown use of unsegregated Federal and State tax funds. The latter would have been absolutely impossible if the cruelly sub-standard situation that has been allowed to evolve and prevail at the Negro asylum had not been cut off from the Bull Street set-up and renamed so as to escape the scrutiny of federal welfare and certifying officials.

    The Governor, apparently greatly shocked by disclosures, assured us that he would investigate conditions as outlined. Since we were continuing our investigation of comparative arrangements for patients at State Park and at Bull Street, we told Governor Russell we would not make our statement public immediately.

    While we know that the Governor will investigate conditions as he has promised, we are forced to assert emphatically that it is the duty of the General Assembly not only to rescind its action in camouflaging the Negro asylum and hiding it away as a family would an afflicted child of whom it is ashamed, but also to send in a Legislative Committee with the demand for a full scale investigation and a report to the public of conditions at State Park.

    Our investigations to date give no evidence that the conditions as outlined by us on December 7 have been alleviated in the least. We call your attention to the following:

    On January 15, many patients were seen running through snow and sleet to and from meals in one garment - no shoes, headgear or coats. They had to gobble in food in this condition, return to their dormitories and allow their garments to dry on their bodies. Reportedly some buildings are chilly.

    Most patients do not have changing apparel and none is available on wards for aids to distribute when necessary. Much clothing is age-old army surplus. Sleeping garments are unheard of - most patients sleeping in apparel worn during the day.

(OVER)

Letter of The Richland County Citizens Committee, Inc. written by Mod-jeska Simkins

Source: https://digital.tcl.sc.edu/digital/collection/mmsimkins/id/11508/rec/4

Neither interest nor regard is shown relative to size, color, or condition of clothing or shoes. A patient wears what can be wheeled out of the MASTER of the supply room. Aids report that they are third-degreed when they request clothing.

Articles necessary for personal hygiene, such as soap, toothpaste, washcloths, towels, etc., for individual patients are unheard of. It is reported that towels have not been seen in the buildings for months. In some wards a dozen washcloths must be shared by thirty patients. Ordinarily, patients bathe and dry themselves with rags sent in for janitorial purposes. If supplies in necessary quantities are delivered to the Negro asylum, "de-ducks" must have massive channels from the supply rooms to parts unknown.

We had believed that the day of the medieval type of asylum or place of bedlam had passed. Certainly through the advances of medical science and the annual expenditure of millions of tax dollars in South Carolina, we should been on the way. The State Negro asylum is bereft of modern benefits, serving only as a place of confinement for patients until they are rescued by oblivion and death.

It is believed that many in official administrative capacities at these outmoded facilities are of the type whose training and social background make them unfit to light even momentarily at the Bull Street facility in any type of job capacity. When it comes to the care of the mentally ill and mentally retarded at State Park and at Pineland, the basic personnel prerequisite is to be white, since professionally trained Negroes are often rejected and untrained whites hired. Integration fades as an issue where a dollar is concerned.

The wilful act of the General Assembly and the Mental Health Commission to fully segregate these facilities has made a botch of the total complex thus creating conditions that must be brought to the attention of federal as well as state authorities and the general public. This state of affairs which is the result of an effort to fully set apart and maneuver by subterfuge so as to appear to have mental facilities fully comparable to those of other States, can only be rectified by complete integration of patients, facilities, and all staffs from top to bottom.

The only comparable parallel to that of conditions at Bull Street and the Negro asylum at State Park would be that of a well-appointed mansion and a filthy hovel.

Respectfully yours,

M. Hester M. M. Simkins

Director of Publicity and Public
Relations

Letter of The Richland County Citizens Committee, Inc. written by Modjeska Simkins (con't)

Modjeska M. Simkins

Modjeska M. Simkins was an important leader in public health reform during the Civil Rights Movement, highlighted the deplorable conditions of the hospital.

A LOOK BACK AT
CRAFTS-FARROW STATE HOSPITAL

From the admission of its first patient in 1828, South Carolina's mental health system was comprised of two state hospitals, first, the South Carolina State Hospital and then the Crafts-Farrow State Hospital.

These hospitals provided care and treatment for people affected by mental illness, mental retardation, aging, and an assortment of behavioral problems.

HISTORY

Major William Crafts

Colonel Samuel Farrow

13460

Images of the History of Crafts-Farrow State Hospital

Source: SC Department of Archives & History

THE HISTORY OF CRAFTS-FARROW STATE HOSPITAL

According to legend, when Colonel Samuel Farrow, a member of the House of Representatives from Spartanburg County, traveled to Columbia to attend sessions of the legislature, he noticed a woman who was mentally distressed and apparently without adequate care. Her poor condition made an impact on him and spurred him on to engage the support of Major William Crafts, a brilliant orator and a member of the Senate from Charleston County.

The two men worked zealously to sensitize their fellow lawmakers to the needs of the mentally ill, and on December 20, 1821, the South Carolina State Legislature passed a statute-at-large approving $30,000 to build the S.C. Lunatic Asylum and school for the death and dumb. This legislation made South Carolina the second state in the nation (after Virginia) to provide funds for the care and treatment of people with mental illnesses.

The hospital admitted patients wealthy enough to pay for their own care, as well as the middle class and paupers. Although a few blacks, mostly slaves, were admitted during the first 20 years, they were not officially permitted until 1848.

With slavery abolished, African-Americans became a larger part of the asylum's population. The admission of blacks not only added to the patient population, but led to another problem-providing separate facilities for the races. Temporary structures built before 1860 for blacks desperately needed replacement. Facilities for whites also were over crowed.

By 1900 the State Hospital had 1,040 patients. More facilities were built in the 1870s and the 1880s. However, the population outgrew these by 1900.

By 1910, after a legislative committee reported the asylum was too small, land was purchased north of Columbia, and plans were submitted for a new complex that became known as "State Park". When it opened in 1913, it was for black patients only. This hospital was named Palmetto State Hospital in 1963, it was renamed Crafts-Farrow State Hospital in 1965 when it became a geriatric facility.

A Potter's field was operated at Crafts-Farrow State Hospital from 1922-1975.

Images of the History of Crafts-Farrow State Hospital (con't)

DEPARTMENT – HEADS (Printed 1973)

Superintendent
Thomas G. Faison, M.D.

Volunteer Services
Mabel P. Hicks

Department of Administration Services
Claude W. Connelley

Supply & Services Division
Robert C. Burrett

Engineering Division
John B. Milling

Housekeeping
La Hugh Majors

Department of Professional Services
Edward M. Burns, M.D.

Residential Care Service
Edward M. Burns, M.D.

Pharmacy Service
Vivian Locklair

Psychology Services
Julian K. Bleeck, PhD

Social Work Services
F. Leon Ellison

Vocational Rehabilitation Service
Earl Pope, III

Personnel Service &
    Employee Relations
Tommie F. Moody

Medical Audit and Evaluations
Helen P. Miller, R.N.

Registrar
W. H. Creech, Jr.

Food Service Division
Bernard A. Cain

Security Division
Clifford Tucker

Fire & Safety
Jack Brown

Admission Exit Service
Thomas G. Cooper, M.D.

Medical-Surgical Service
Karl M. Lippert, M.D.

Nursing Service
Barbara J. Thomas, R.N.

Activity Therapy Service
Devert Moore

Chaplaincy Service
William Major

Excerpts for this history were obtained from "South Carolina Department of History and Archives, South Carolina Department of Mental Health, Susan Craft, and SCDMH Office of Public Affairs, and interviews with former employees of Crafts-Farrow State Hospital."

Research information was compiled by Ms. Irma A. Patterson and Mrs. Claretha B. Free. The history of Crafts-Farrow State Hospital was written by Mrs. Claretha B. Free.

Images of the History of Crafts-Farrow State Hospital (con't)

Floster L. Ellison, Jr. is listed under "Social Work Services"

Social Workers Visit Greenville, S. C.:

On October 25, 1967, Miss Cynthia Taylor, Mr. Floster Ellison, Mr. Thomas Davis, and Mr. Otis Corbitt, attended the annual meeting of the Department of Mental Health, Greenville, S. C. The leading speaker was Dr. Alan I. Levenson, Director of the Divisional of Mental Health. Other speakers were Dr. Ronald Young, Dr. Nicala Kaft and Dr. George Buch.

The Variety Newsletter, Vol. 15, Nos.10-11, October–November 1967

In this artilce, Floster L. Ellison, Jr., along with his nephew, Dr. Otis Corbitt, and colleagues attended an annual meeting of the Department of Mental Health in Greenville, SC.

Source: South Carolina State Library

APPENDIX XX–THE STALEY BROTHERS

A few years later, after the death of his father in 1945, Tommy became a lead singer for the Staley Brothers, a local gospel quartet from Salley, South Carolina. The Staley Brothers were part of the African American quartet tradition of gospel music that originated at Fisk University, an historic African American university located in Nashville, Tennessee in 1871. During that year, Fisk University formed the Fisk Jubilee Singers, a student choir that went on tour to raise money for university, which was facing financial challenges. African American gospel quartets generally have four to six members, with instrumentation that allows for more voices to be added, including a lead singer. The lead singers would add personal testimonies to their music. Another characteristic among African American quartet groups is improvisation in the form of ad-libbing, dance movements, acting, and crowd participation.

This section includes:

1. Pictures of the Staley Brothers
2. Picture of Rosa Hill Missionary Baptist Church

Eugene W. Staley

Paul Staley, Jr.

Rev. Matthew Staley

Lester Staley, Sr.

The Staley Brothers

The Staley Brothers included brothers Lester Staley, Sr., Matthew Staley, Eugene W. Staley, and Paul Staley, Jr., along with members Luther Evans and Bill Johnson. The brothers were members of Friendship Baptist Church of Salley, South Carolina.

Rosa Hill Missionary Baptist Church

Wagener, South Carolina

The Staley Brothers held performances at various venues across Aiken County, notably Gum Ridge School, Red Hill Baptist Church, and Rosa Hill Missionary Baptist Church. Their average concert attendance was between forty and fifty people, and they charged guests forty cents, sometimes higher, depending on the venue.

XXI–Tommy Ellison and the Five Singing Stars

Tommy Ellison & the Five Singing Stars recorded under several record labels, including Revelation, Peacock Records, HOB, HSE Records, and Atlantic International Records. The quartet released a string of successful albums including "Closer," "Born Again," "Going to See My Friend," "Come Home," "Power," "Let This Be A Lesson To You," and well-known singles, including "Trying to Get to Heaven," "Pity in the City," "Let This Be A Lesson to You" (Drunk Driver), and "On My Way To Grandma House." They performed across the country, started a fan club, and regularly appeared on radio and television and performed at New York City's renowned venues: Madison Square Garden, Apollo Theater, and Carnegie Hall.

This section includes:

1. A picture of of Tommy Ellison and the Five Singing Stars
2. Covers of Tommy Ellison and the Five Singing Stars most popular albums and singles
3. A picture of the Legendary Singing Stars
4. "Gospel Concert Features Diverse Talent at Hillside" newspaper article
5. "Gospel Not The Same, But He Still Likes It" newspaper article
6. "Glorious Gospel" newspaper article
7. A South Carolina House of Representatives Resolution sponsored by Rep. John Scott to recongize Tommy Ellison & The Singing Stars

TOMMY ELLISON
and the world famous 5 Singing Stars

Manager
Charlie Baker
122-44 Grayson St.
St. Albans, L.I., N.Y.
(212) 528 - 2848

Tommy Ellison & The Five Singing Stars

Upon Charlie's recommendation, based on Tommy's experience, leadership, and notoriety, in 1960, the group renamed itself "Tommy Ellison and the Five Singing Stars." Members of the quartet at one time or another included Charlie Baker, Billy Hardie, Dennis Bowers, Joe Dawkins Jr., Franklin "Big O" Hardnett, Justin Mickens, Joseph Ricks Horns, Sam Moses, Sam Williams, and Perry Taft.

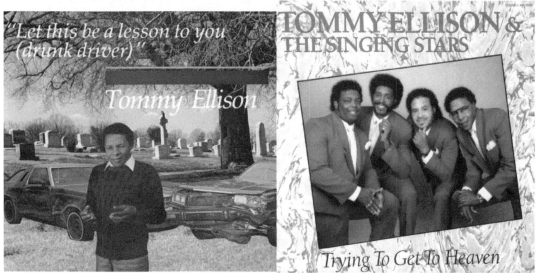

Covers of Tommy Ellison and the Five Singing Stars most popular albums & singles

Tommy Ellison & Five Singing Stars recorded under several record labels, including Revelation, Peacock Records, HOB, HSE Records, and Atlantic International Records. The quartet released a string of successful albums including "Closer," "Born Again," "Going to See My Friend," "Come Home," "Power," "Let This Be A Lesson To You," and well-known singles, including "Trying to Get to Heaven," "Pity in the City," "Let This Be A Lesson to You" (Drunk Driver), and "On My Way To Grandma House.

The Legendary Singing Stars

The Legendary Singing Stars, originally called Tommy Ellison & Five Singing Stars of Brooklyn, NY. Founding member and former lead singer Tommy Ellison, who passed away in 2009.

James Davis, lead singer of Arthur Crume and the Soool Stirrers, Valerie Bailey, president of the Tommy Ellison and the Five Singing Stars Fan Club, Inc., Gloria Robinson, treasurer of the club, and E.W. Moore, a gospel singer, are readying for the gospel concert this Saturday at Hillside School. Doors open at 7 P.M.

Gospel Concert Features Diverse Talent At Hillside

The Tommy Ellison and the Five Singing Stars Fan Club, Inc., will celebrate its second anniversary with a gospel concert Saturday night at Hillside School.

Special guests include Arthur Crume and the World Famous Soul Stirrers of Chicago, Ill., Clarence Fountain and the

brates

Anniversary

After many transitions, the Rev. Lincoln McGee, the present pastor, received and accepted the

Five Blind Boys of Alabama, and E.W. Moore of Little Washington, N.C.

Also appearing will be Tommy Ellison and the Five Singing Stars. The emcee for the program will be Don "Early" Allen of WWRL radio, Woodside, N.Y.

The Tommy Ellison and the Five Singing Stars Fan Club, Inc., is a non-profit organization founded in June of 1981. The club's primary goal is to promote the Tommy Ellison group and other gospel singers.

The fan club has

travelled with the Tommy Ellison group to promote it and set up branch offices for the fan club.

Doors open at 7 P.M. and admission is $10 for adults in advance, $12 at the door and $3 at the door for children under 12.

For more information or reservations call 744-7508, 744-9204, or 744-0240.

The word "cigar" was coined from th word "cicada" because the first cigars supposedly looked like beetles.

"Gospel Concert Features Diverse Talent at Hillside", The Montclair Times, Montclair, New Jersey, September 8th, 1963

In this article, highlights the work of Tommy Ellison & Five Singing Stars Fan Club, Inc who traveled with Tommy Ellison & Five Singing Stars whose job was to promote it and set up branch offices for the fan club

Source: https://www.newspapers.com/clip/64122142/tommy-ellison-fan-club-1981/

Gospel's Not the Same, But He Still Likes It

Thermon Ruth

THE PROBLEM IN black gospel quartet singing today, says Thermon Ruth, has less to do with the music than the audience.

"People don't want reality today," says Ruth, who turned 73 in March and has been singing quartet-style gospel since his church days in Brooklyn in the 1920s. "They want a show. It's the same as if I told you I would sell you magic pills from the South that would cure your headache, and you'd pay $5 apiece for 'em. But if I told you they were just aspirin, which does the same thing for a penny or two, you wouldn't be interested.

"With gospel quartet singing, you sit and listen and you

get the truth. Short and sweet and not too loud. But a lot of folks don't want that. Instead of a bass, they want a whole choir. They say, 'Let's have church,' as if you have to roll

INTERVIEW

in the aisle. A lot of it is too much like rock 'n' roll to me."

Ironically, Ruth plays modern gospel on his radio show over WNYM. But his heart, as you may gather, lies with the traditional quartet sound, the one he traces in his own life back to the Charioteers, the Golden Gate Quartet and the Norfolk Jubilee Singers.

So it's the traditional music he'll be presenting Sunday at the Apollo Theater, when his Tri-Gospel Associates spon-

sors a 2 p.m. show featuring the Swanee Quintet, Tommy Ellison & the Five Singing Stars, Clarence Fountain and the Five Blind Boys of Alabama, R.H. Harris, the Rev. Claude Jeter and others—including, possibly, a reunion among some surviving members of Ruth's own famous Selah Jubilee Singers.

It's the Selahs for which Ruth left Brooklyn those many years ago. "I got a rich musical upbringing here."

After the Selahs had spent time on the gospel circuit, which was not exactly a life of ease, they worked their way to Raleigh, N.C., where they got a 15-minute daily program on 50,000-watt station WPTF. "We got into town with $6

among us," says Ruth.

Besides their gospel work, the Selahs also eventually made a mark in rhythm and blues, renaming themselves the Larks and cutting a series of classics for the Apollo label in the early '50s.

"You had to be careful," Ruth says. "If your gospel fans knew you were doing pop, they'd be upset. But I think you can sing both."

It was Ruth who convinced Apollo owner Frank Schiffman to start putting on gospel programs. "He wasn't sure the audience would accept gospel," Ruth recalls. "But they did, right from the first show. The Selahs sang on that one. So did the Pilgrim Travelers, when Lou Rawls was with them."

—David Hinckley

"Gospel Not The Same, But He Still Likes It", Daily News, New York, New York, July 18th, 1987

In this article, mentions Tommy Ellion & Five Singing Stars performance at the Apollo Theatre in Harlem, New York.

Source: https://www.newspapers.com/clip/60712139/tommy-ellison-apollo-theatre/

Glorious gospel

Legendary Singing Stars bring 5 decades of tradition to Grey Eagle

By Jedd Ferris | Scene Correspondent

ASHEVILLE — The Legendary Singing Stars are bringing more than 50 years of high-energy gospel tradition to The Grey Eagle on Sunday evening.

Back in the '60s, the Brooklyn, N.Y.-born band was regularly packing the Apollo Theatre, and the group went on to play additional famed venues in New York City, including Carnegie Hall and Madison Square Garden.

After five decades, they're still at it — delivering the good word through tight soulful jams and a captivating live act that keeps crowds moving to joyful noise.

Think James Brown grooves and dance moves with homage to a higher power.

Not your typical church music

The Legendary Singing Stars play gospel quartet music, which adds elements of blues, funk and R&B to traditional gospel.

"It's a very exciting electric show — not your typical church music," says Steve Mann, a long-time fan and occasional local music promoter responsible for bringing the band back to town after nearly a decade. "Anyone who likes blues or funk or soul will appreciate this show."

The band was originally called Tommy Ellison and the Five Singing Stars of Brooklyn, N.Y. Founding member and former lead singer Tommy Ellison, who passed away last year, sang with Sam Cooke in the 1950s.

In addition to his work with gospel legends like Shirley Caesar and Lee Williams, Ellison is known as a pioneer who helped gospel crossover by giving it a soulful electric edge.

Longtime Singing Stars Sam Williams, Franklin "Big O" Hardnett and Dennis Bowers are carrying the torch, touring with a big-band ensemble that includes four singers, three guitars, two keyboardists and a rhythm section.

"They're still out there doing it, because this is the music they love," says Mann. "I think we're all a little richer for it."

Moving into clubs

These days the Singing Stars, whose members now mostly reside in South Carolina, are predominantly playing in churches in schools. But with bands like the Blind Boys of Alabama and the Mighty Clouds of Joy playing national club gigs, Mann thinks The Grey Eagle is the perfect venue for the Singing Stars.

In addition to infectious grooves, the band adds to their live show with matching tailored suits and choreographed dance moves.

"It's the same genre as the Blind Boys of Alabama, but it's more raw," Mann says of Stars' sound. "It's going to be really fun music for a club."

Jedd Ferris writes about entertainment for takeS. Email him at jeddferris@gmail.com.

Special to the Citizen-Times
The Legendary Singing Stars perform Sunday at The Grey Eagle Music Hall.

"Glorious Gospel", Asheville Citizen-Times, Asheville, North Carolina, March 28, 2010

In this artilce, highlights the Legendary Singing Stars legacy and performance at The Grey Eagle in Asheville, North Carolina. The article also highlights Tommy Ellison work with gospel legends that included Shirley Casear and Lee Williams.

Source: https://www.newspapers.com/clip/74558373/glorious-gospel/

A HOUSE RESOLUTION

TO RECOGNIZE TOMMY ELLISON AND THE SINGING STARS FOR THEIR OUT-STANDING CONTRIBUTION TOWARD PRESERVING THE HERITAGE OF AFRICAN AMERICAN GOSPEL MUSIC, SPREADING KNOWLEDGE AND LOVE OF THIS MUSICAL TREASURE, AND CREATING NEW AUDIENCES FOR ITS ENJOYMENT.

Whereas, gospel music is an integral part of the cultural fiber of South Carolina and the United States and, more particularly, of the African American community; and

Whereas, the history of gospel music and the African American community are interwoven in such a way that the music has often reflected the struggles, challenges, and victories of the African American community; and

Whereas, as part of the gospel music industry for more than fifty years, Tommy Ellison and The Singing Stars, founded by Echo native "The Superstar" Mr. Tommy Ellison, are one of the most sought-after gospel groups to tour this country; and

Whereas, although blessed to call the United States home, Tommy Ellison and The Singing Stars perform well beyond its boundaries, possessing a well-deserved worldwide reputation as one of the best gospel groups ever to sing the Good News of Jesus. Now, therefore,

Be it resolved by the House of Representatives:

That the members of the South Carolina House of Representatives, by this resolution, recognize Tommy Ellison and The Singing Stars for their outstanding contribution toward preserving the heritage of African American gospel music, spreading knowledge and love of this musical treasure, and creating new audiences for its enjoyment.

Be it further resolved that a copy of this resolution be presented to Tommy Ellison and The Singing Stars.

A South Carolina House of Representatives Resolution sponsored by Rep. John Scott to recongize Tommy Ellison & The Singing Stars

Source: https://www.scstatehouse.gov/sess117_2007-2008/bills/3860.htm

XXII—The Brick Masonry Work of Roosevelt & Henry Seawright

In 1957, Roosevelt pursued the tradesmen craft of brick masonry as a helper; then in 1960, he became a brick mason. As a brick mason, Roosevelt was a very skilled and experienced tradesperson who laid bricks and blocks without supervision and provided supervision to less-skilled workers. He was employed with Gents and Associates, Schaeffer Builders, and Bill Gainer Builders. He did brick work throughout the Aiken area, Beech Island, Jackson, and North Augusta, South Carolina. He bricked his own home and homes in several prominent communities, which included Governs Acres and Gatewood Subdivision. Roosevelt, along with his brother Henry, is credited with the building of Montmorenci Missionary Baptist Church, which is in Montmorenci, east of Aiken, and Smith Hazel Recreational Center, located at 400 Kershaw Street in Aiken and named after Josie Hazel and Jason Smith, who were community activists who gave money to build it.

This section includes pictures of the homes and facilities that Roosevelt and Henry bricked:

1. The family home of Roosevelt & Louise J. Seawright
2. The family home of Renee Seawright, daughter of Roosevelt & Louise J. Seawright
3. The family home of Linda Jenkins, niece of Roosevelt & Louise J. Seawright
4. A Neigborhood Home
5. Montmorenci Missionary Baptist Church
6. Smith Hazel Recreational Center

The family home of Roosevelt & Louise J. Seawright

Aiken, South Carolina

The family home of Renee Seawright, daughter of Roosevelt & Louise J. Seawright

Aiken, South Carolina

The family home of Linda Jenkins Barnwell, niece of Roosevelt & Louise J. Seawright

Aiken, South Carolina

A Neighborhood Home

Aiken, South Carolina

Montmorenci Missionary Baptist Church

Aiken, South Carolina

Smith-Hazel Recreation Center

Aiken, South Carolina

XXIII– WASHINGTON STREET BUSINESS DISTRICT–COLUMBIA'S BLACK WALL STREET

A few years after the end of World War II, Floster L. Ellison, Jr. began his illustrious career in professional barbering. He started working at a local barbershop located in downtown Columbia, SC, under the supervision of Mr. Smith. In 1947, Floster partnered with his friend, Joseph Stroy, and they opened their own barbershop named Ellison & Stroy, located in the historic Columbia African American business district along Washington Street before the Civil Rights Movement.

This section includes:

1. The history of Washington Street Business District-Columbia's "Black Wall Street"
2. A picture of Columbia Black Wall Street Building
3. A picture of Joseph Stroy, business partner of Floster L. Ellison, Jr.

The history of Washington Street Business District-Columbia's "Black Wall Street"

From Reconstruction through the Civil Rights Era, many cities around the country had Black Business Districts, also referred to as "Black Wall Streets." Some, such as those in Tulsa, Oklahoma and Knoxville, Tennessee, were destroyed by race riots. Others fell victim to the ravages of time and integration.

In Columbia, the area around Washington Street from Assembly to Gadsden Street was known as Columbia's "Black Wall Street." For nearly a century, hundreds of thriving Black-owned businesses supplied goods and services to the Black community. There were Black-owned grocery stores, theaters, insurance companies, funeral homes, attorneys – no matter what you needed, there was probably a Black-owned business in Columbia's Black Wall Street available to supply it.

The businesses in the district included: Angeline's Wig & Beauty Supply, Blue Palace Barbershop, Counts Drug Store, Elise Martin Beauty Salon, Jack's Lunch, Joe's Barber Shop, Koon's Tea Room, Nell's Moon Glow, Owens & Paul Tailoring, Pearson Funeral Home, Richardson Cleaners, Robinson Enterprises, Stroy Barber Shop, Society Beauty Shop, and T.H. Pinckney Undertaker Company.

Today, there are thousands of Black-owned businesses spread throughout the city and across the Midlands. But the roots of Columbia's Black businesses can be traced to Washington Street.

Source: www.carolinapanorma.com

Columbia Black Wall Street Building

Corner of Washington & Assembly Street
Columbia, South Carolina

The Columbia Black Will Street building was on the corner of Washington and Assembly Streets that housed Angeline's Beauty Supply, the last remaining business from that era, was bulldozed to make room for an apartment complex.

Source: www.carolinapanorma.com

Joseph Stroy, business partner of Floster L. Ellison, Jr.,

Floster L. Ellison, Jr. and Joseph Stroy co-owned Ellison & Stroybbarbershop, which was located in the Columbia Black Wall District on the corner of Washington & Assembly streets in downtown Columbia, South Carolina. They charged seventy-five cents for haircuts and twenty-five cents for mustache and beard grooming, and they employed barbers who they charged ten percent from their profits for rent and other expenses.

Source: www.carolinapanorma.com

APPENDIX XXIV–THE WAVERLY COMMUNITY

For the first few years, Floster L. Ellison, Jr., and his family lived in the historic Waverly community, designated as Columbia's first suburb. Waverly was a progressive community of African Americans that included artisans, professionals, and social reformers who were instrumental in the social and political advancement of Africans Americans in Columbia and South Carolina.

This section includes:

1. A history of the Waverly Community
2. A picture of Floster L. Ellison Waverly Community home and an image of his address.

A history of the Waverly Community

Waverly has been one of Columbia's most significant black communities since the 1930s. The city's first residential suburb, it grew out of a 60-acre parcel bought by Robert Latta in 1855. Latta's widow and children sold the first lots here in 1863. Shortly after the Civil War, banker and textile manufacturer Lysander D. Childs bought several blocks here for development. Waverly grew for the next 50 years. The City of Columbia annexed Waverly in 1913. Two black colleges, Benedict College and Allen University, drew many African Americans to this area as whites moved away. By the 1930s this community was almost entirely black.

Waverly evolved into a self-contained, self-sustaining black community with a broad socio-economic demographic. Girded by the presence of two colleges, myriad of churches, a hospital and nurse training facility, as well as numerous stores and small businesses, Waverly featured many middle- and upper-class African American residents, many of whom were leaders within spiritual, business, academic, and professional circles, as well as those in the service industries. Over time, this community expanded to encompass the streets south of Gervais Street. Those streets included the homes of many civil rights activists, including George A. Elmore.

The Waverly Historic District, bounded by Gervais, Harden, and Taylor Streets and Millwood Avenue, was listed in the National Register of Historic Places in 1989.

Source: https://greenbookofsc.com/locations/waverly/
Source: https://www.historiccolumbia.org/tour-locations/2300-lady-street

Floster L. Ellison, Jr. Waverly Community Home

1202 Oak Street
Columbia, South Carolina
The house was constructed in 1913.
Source: http://nationalregister.sc.gov/richland/S10817740098/index.htm

" Floster L jr (Marie) barber C Luther
" Lilliewood r1202 Oak

Floster L. Ellison, Jr. Waverly Community Address

In this record, Floster address is "r1202 Oak" which is the same Oak Street today.
Source: Ancestry.com. U.S., City Directories, 1822–1995.

APPENDIX XXV–THE GREENVIEW COMMUNITY

Tired of renting, Floster L. Ellison, Jr., and his family achieved the dream of homeownership and relocated permanently to the newly established Greenview Community, a suburb in northern Columbia that was once a cow pasture and a planned community for African American veterans, like Floster, returning from World War II, who were given opportunities to buy homes for their families in the community. Floster opened his barbershop in the community shopping center, in addition to several barbershops and a beauty salon he also owned. In conjunction with furthering his pursuits, Floster was instrumental in the organization of Greenview First Baptist Church, where he served as a deacon and church treasurer and later became the first president of Fairwold Junior High School Parents Teachers Association.

This section includes:

1. A picture of Floster L. Ellison, Jr., first Greenview Community home and an image of his address.
2. A picture of Floster L. Ellison, Jr., second Greenview Community home
3. A picture of Greenview First Baptist Church
4. A brief history of Fairwold Junior High School

Floster L. Ellison, Jr., First Greenview Community Home

600 Wilkes Street
Columbia, South Carolina

' Floster L jr (Marie) social wkr State Hosp r600
Wilkes rd

Floster L. Ellison, Jr., First Greenview Community Home Address

In this record, Floster address is "r600 Wilkes rd" which is the same Wilkes Rd today.

Source: Ancestry.com. U.S., City Directories, 1822-1995.

Floster L. Ellison, Jr., Second Greenview Community Home

706 Juniper Street
Columbia, South Carolina

Name:	Floster J Ellison
Birth Date:	10 Oct 1922
Address:	706 Juniper St
Residence Place:	Columbia, South Carolina, USA
Zip Code:	29203-5059

Floster L. Ellison, Jr., Second Greenview Community Address

Source: Ancestry.com. U.S., City Directories, 1822-1995.

Greenview First Baptist Church

On October 19, 1953, Greenview First Baptist was chartered by the State of South Carolina for the purpose of operating as a church in accordance with the Baptist faith. The Executive Board of the Gethsemane Association organized Greenview First Baptist Church on December 29, 1953. The groundbreaking service for the original building was held on the First Sunday in January 1953. The first service in the new building was held January 24, 1954. Reverend J.W. Davis served as the first pastor until January 1959. Floster L. Ellison, Jr., served as deacon and church treasurer.

Source: https://www.greenviewfirstbaptistchurch.org/history/

Fairwold Junior High School, 1961

William G. Sanders
Principal 1965–1983

Fairwold Junior High School was built at 6000 Alida Street in 1961 for $594,829. The 15.6 acres of land had been purchased for $47,617. The contractor was Spong Construction Company; the architect was Tom Harmon & Associates. Original equipment cost $88,900.

The school had four separate wings. The interior consisted of 18 modern classrooms, laboratories, a cafetorium, office, first-aid room, student activity room, band room, music room, industrial arts room, library, journalism room, physical education locker rooms, and two well-equipped home economics rooms.

The school opened September, 1961, with 525 students who transferred from W.A. Perry Junior High. It was the second junior high for negro students in Columbia. Stoney M. Richburg was the principal. The faculty included Mrs. E. Clyburn, Lucius Frierson, J. Lindsey, Mrs. T. Bomar Shaw, Mrs. E. Davis, George Lawson, Miss D. Gordon, Mrs. H. Smith Adams, Mrs. P. Sweat, Mr. Galloway, Miss Haynes, W.R. Snoden, Miss E. Friday, J. Stephens, Miss Howard, Mrs. S. Babridge, Miss R. Wright, Cecil Adderly, Ernest Henderson, Mrs. Elizabeth Blackman, Mrs. L. King, Miss Catherine Pelot, James Hardy Jr., Agnes Atkisson, Susie Freeman, and Thelma M. Harrison. Miss Willie Reid was the secretary.

Jasper Salmond was the school's business manager and taught math and science. Some of the students in his first class were Doris Cannon, Linda Reese, Willie Bryan, and John Brown. Salmond became Fairwold's first assistant principal in 1963. He was succeeded by W.R. Stockman in 1970. Stockman retired in 1976 after 37 years in Columbia City Schools.

The words for the alma mater were written by James Sanders, a seventh grade student. Music was adapted by Lillian Ray. The first student body president was Harned Gaitor. Floster Ellison was the first PTA president. Rev. Wendell Able was vice president; Gracie Gist, secretary; and John Bailey, treasurer.

A Brief History of Fairwold Junior High School

Floster L. Ellison, Jr. was the first PTA president of the school (see highlighted)

Source: https://localhistory.richlandlibrary.com/digital/collection/p16817coll11

APPENDIX XXVI–THE GRANITEVILLE MANUFACTURING COMPANY

On June 2, 1964, President Lydon B. Johnson signed the Civil Rights Act of 1964, which outlawed discrimination based on race, color, religion, sex, national origin, and sexual orientation and prohibited employment discrimination. A few years after the law was enacted, the South's largest industry, textile manufacturing, underwent radical changes in the racial composition of its workforce. Previously, African Americans were barred from textile mill jobs, but that ended under the act. In South Carolina, less than five percent of mill employees were African American in 1964.

Between 1960 and 1969, African Americans employment in textile mills increased four times faster than the national average for all manufacturing. In 1969, Wallace Seawright, Sr., was employed as a draw frame operator at the Hickman Mill of the Graniteville Manufacturing Company, a major textile manufacturing company located in Graniteville, South Carolina, until his retirement in 1982.

This section includes:

1. The history of the Graniteville Manufacturing Company
2. Pictures of the Hickman Division Mill
3. A picture of a drawing frame at Hickman Division Mill
4. An image of Wallace Seawright, Sr. Retirement Announcement
5. "Hickman Mill Being Expanded" newspaper article
6. A picture of H.H. Hickman

The history of the Graniteville Manufacturing Company

Chartered by the South Carolina General Assembly in December 1845, the Graniteville Company was one of the earliest and most successful textile manufacturing operations in the South. The guiding light behind its creation was William Gregg, a highly successful Charleston jeweler-turned-manufacturer who became a leading proponent of southern industrialization during the antebellum era. With an initial capitalization of $300,000 raised primarily from the Charleston mercantile community, the company commenced operations in 1849 in a massive granite factory located on the banks of Horse Creek in southern Edgefield District (now Aiken County). After some initial teething, the company quickly proved highly prosperous, producing shirting and sheeting that sold well in markets as far away as Philadelphia and New York. Graniteville was also unusual in that it employed the labor of free white laborers, mostly women and teenaged children, at a time when most southern manufacturers used the labor of black slaves. During the Civil War, Graniteville produced cloth for the Confederate government as well as the civilian market. It was also one of the few southern manufacturing companies to survive the war largely intact and resumed civilian production shortly after the end to hostilities.

The Graniteville Company expanded in the decades following the war, building new factories at neighboring Vaucluse and Warrenville and acquiring two mills (Sibley and Enterprise) in nearby Augusta, Georgia. Declining profits forced the company into receivership briefly in 1915, but it emerged in just seventeen months, thanks to government orders brought about by America's entry into World War I. The 1920s and 1930s were lean years for Graniteville, with increasing competition and the Great Depression taking a toll on company profits. War orders during the 1940s again improved the fortunes of the company, allowing the company to pay off all its debts and embark on a massive postwar modernization plan. In the years following the war, Graniteville Company pioneered the production of permanent-press textiles. Acquired by Avondale Mills, Inc., in 1996, the remaining Graniteville facilities continued to produce high quality denim, cotton, and specialty fabrics.

Source: www.scencyclopedia.org

Hickman Division Mill of the Graniteville Manufacturing Company at Day

Hickman Division Mill of the Graniteville Manufacturing Company at Night

Source: Courtesy of the Gregg-Graniteville Archives, Gregg-Graniteville Library, University of South Carolina Aiken, Aiken, South Carolina.

Drawing frame with silver cans at the Hickman Division Mill

Draw frame operators operated the draw frame machine, ensured proper feeding of carded or combed sliver, pieced the sliver on breakage, doffed the sliver cans, and transported the delivery cans to the storage area. This job required the individual to have thorough knowledge of process flow and material flow in a textile mill for yarn production, and they had to know the important functions and operations of all the machines in drawing department.

Source: Courtesy of the Gregg-Graniteville Archives, Gregg-Graniteville Library, University of South Carolina Aiken, Aiken, South Carolina.

Wallace Seawright was a draw frame operator at Hickman when he retired in August after 13 years of service.

Wallace Seawright, Sr. Retirement Announcement

Source: Graniteville Bulletin, Sept/Oct 1982

HICKMAN MILL BEING EXPANDED

Hickman Mill is "coming right along," according to William E. Johnson, assistant vice president of administration at Graniteville Company. The preliminary expansion work is done, and Hickman Street is closed to traffic. The mill, which will employ 90 to 100 people, will manufacture heavy weight fabric for slacks. Johnson said the "addition will help balance finishing and manufacturing." The new portion will open in the summer of 1976.

"Hickman Mill Being Expanded", Aiken Standard, Aiken, South Carolina, June 7ᵗʰ, 1974

During Wallace's tenure at Graniteville, in 1976, the Hickman Mill instituted a 10 million expansion program that added 100 jobs to the company, 6,000 positions at that time.

Source: https://www.newspapers.com/clip/61934590/hickman-mill-being-expanded-aiken/

WILLIAM GREGG.

William Gregg

Founder and first president of the Graniteville

Manufacturing Company

(1800-1867)

Hamilton H. Hickman

Hamilton H. Hickman was the second president of the Graniteville Manufacturing Company (1867-1899).

Source: Courtesy of the Gregg-Graniteville Archives, Gregg-Graniteville Library, University of South Carolina Aiken, Aiken, South Carolina.

APPENDIX XXVII–THE SAWYERDALE COMMUNITY

The years (1918-1921), Furman Seawright and his family lived in Sawyerdale, whose citizens and institutions were civically and socially active. Institutions such as the Sawyerdale library and the Sawyerdale school were bastions of community life. During World War 1 (1914-1918), men from Sawyerdale joined the military and after the war, the community memorialized the fallen soldiers for their service and sacrifice. A few months before the United States entered the war in 1918, the Sawyerdale community mourned the death of their native son, Carlton Wilkes Sawyer, who served as South Carolina Comptroller General. In 1920, Sawyerdale citizens D.S Sawyer, C.P Reed, and C.O Daughterty, publicly endorsed Springfield native, Hampton P. Fulmer for Congress, who served in the S.C House of Representatives and was elected to Congress. While Sawyerdale and the surrounding communities successfully elected Fulmer to Congress in the general election of 1920, the infamous poll tax disenfranchised African Americans and poor whites from voting in Sawyerdale and across the county and state.

This section includes the following newspaper articles and sources that corroborated the aforementioned information along with other pertinent information:

1. A picture of the Saywerdale community sign
2. A brief history of the Sawyerdale library
3. A picture of the Sawyerdale School & map
4. "Sawyerdale News" newspaper articles
5. "Memorial Services" newspaper article
6. "Sawyerdale Memorial Services Last Sunday" newspaper article
7. "Universal Sorrow" newspaper article
8. "Funeral Last Sunday" newspaper article
9. "Fulmer Endorsed By His Neighbors" newspaper article
10. "Jiggs at Home Will Be Seen at Sawyerdale" newspaper article
11. "Notice of Election" newspaper article

The Sawyerdale Community Sign

The Sawyerdale community located in western Orangeburg County between Neeses, South Carolina and the Orangeburg/Aiken County line.

SAWYERDALE   19L

SAWYERDALE LIBRARY IS OLDEST OF KIND IN U. S...

Sawyerdale, April 16. - According to the WPA library
records, the Sawyerdale library, which was started in 1907,
has the distinction of being the oldest rural library in
the United States.

The library was delighted to have as a visitor recently Mrs. Mary T. Nance Daniel of Greenwood. She, as Miss
Mary T. Nance, assisted Mrs. Ollie H. Schoenberg in organ-
izing this library at old Julia Academy, which was later
consolidated into Sawyerdale. Mrs. Daniel and Mrs. Schoenberg visited Julia Academy near Miss Viola Sharpe's home-
stead recently and from there they came to the new, handsome brick structure at Sawyerdale. They marveled at the
progress that has been made.

The Board of Trustees, consisting of J. B. Boles,
Leroy Jeffcoat and Ottis O. Williamson, are now applying
for a charter for this unit, which will be named the Mary
T. Nance Daniel Library..

It is very fitting to give this distinction of Mrs.
Daniels as she is a great leader in the educational life
of this state. For quiteawhile, she was president of the
state School Improvement Association. She is now a trustee
of Winthrop College and also a valued member of the faculty of the Greenwood city schools.

T. & D., 17 Apr 1941(Thurs.)

Brief history of the Sawyerdale Library

According to the WPA (Works Progress Administration) records, the Sawyerdale library, which
was started in 1907, has the distinction of being the oldest rural library in the United States.

Source: Courtesy of Orangeburg County Historical Society

Sawyerdale School

The Sawyerdale School, located in the Sawyerdale community, served White elementary students in during the era of racial segregation.

Source: http://www.nationalregister.sc.gov/

Map of Sawyerdale School

The Sawyerdale School was originally located on the land that corners SC Hwy 3 and 389 in the Sawyerdale community.

Source: Courtesy of Orangeburg County Historical Society

"Sawyerdale News", The Times & Democrat, May 25, 1918

In this article mentions Mr. H.R. Schoenberg effort to engage African Americans in the Sawyerdale community and the noted enthusiasm of African Americans to be engaged.

Source: https://www.newspapers.com/clip/75218431/sawyerdale-news/

"Sawyerdale News", The Times & Democrat, May 11, 1918

In this article mentioned "the Red Cross branch of Sawyerdale has undertaken the making of sixteen pajamas".

Source: https://www.newspapers.com/clip/75036541/sawyerdale-news-times-and-democrat/

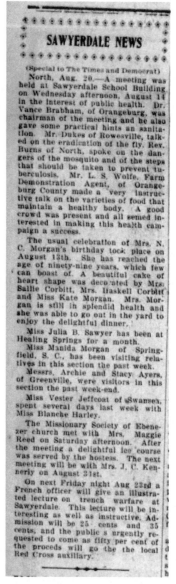

SAWYERDALE NEWS

(Special to The Times and Democrat)

North, Aug. 20.—A meeting was held at Sawyerdale School Building on Wednesday afternoon, August 14 in the interest of public health. Dr. Vance Brabham, of Orangeburg, was chairman of the meeting and he also gave some practical hints on sanitation. Mr. Dukes of Rowesville, talked on the eradication of the fly. Rev. Burns of North, spoke on the dangers of the mosquito and of the steps that should be taken to prevent tuberculosis. Mr. L. S. Wolfe, Farm Demonstration Agent, of Orangeburg County made a very instructive talk on the varieties of food that maintain a healthy body. A good crowd was present and all semed interested in making this health campaign a success.

The usual celebration of Mrs. N. C. Morgan's birthday took place on August 13th. She has reached the age of ninety-nine years, which few can boast of. A beautiful cake of heart shape was decorated by Mrs. Sallie Corbitt, Mrs. Haskell Corbitt and Miss Kate Morgan. Mrs. Morgan is still in splendid health and she was able to go out in the yard to enjoy the delightful dinner.

Miss Julia B. Sawyer has been at Healing Springs for a month.

Miss Manida Morgan of Springfield, S. C., has been visiting relatives in this section the past week.

Messrs. Archie and Stacy Ayers, of Greenville, were visitors in this section the past week-end.

Miss Vester Jeffcoat of Swansea, spent several days last week with Miss Blanche Harley.

The Missionary Society of Ebenezer church met with Mrs. Maggie Reed on Saturday afternoon. After the meeting a delightful ice course was served by the hostess. The next meeting will be with Mrs. J. C. Kennerly on August 31st.

On next Friday night Aug 23rd a French officer will give an illustrated lecture on trench warfare at Sawyerdale. This lecture will be interesting as well as instructive. Admission will be 25 cents and 35 cents, and the public is urgently requested to come as fifty per cent of the proceds will go the the local Red Cross auxiliary.

"Sawyerdale News", The Times & Democrat, August 24, 1918

In this article, a meeting was held at Sawyerdale school on a series of public health topics from leading experts in Orangeburg County. The article also announced that a French officer was scheduled to give a lecture on trench warfare during World War I.

Source: https://www.newspapers.com/clip/62310698/sawyerdale-news-the-times-and/

MEMORIAL SERVICES

Exercises Will Be Held at Orangeburg, Sawyerdale and Ebenezer Sunday in Interest of Memorial.

Memorial services to men of Orangeburg County who lost their lives in the service during the War are to be held at Ebenezer Church, near Bowman and at Sawyerdale, Sunday October 19th. There will also be a service held in Orangeburg on the grounds of the First Baptist Church at six o'clock in the afternoon of the same day.

The services at Ebenezer Church will be held at 11 A. M., and are especially for the Cow Castle section of the county. Lieutenant Governor Junius T. Lyles will deliver the Memorial address. The committees in charge of the Memorial Fund campaign in this district are as follows: Woman's Comittee, Mrs. Jessie Whetsell, Chairman, Misses Nettie Wannamaker, Myrtle Lee Bozard, and Jessie Bell; Mens Committee, Mr. T. P. Whetsell, Chairman, and Messrs. J. L. Huff, Arthur Whetsell, W. S. Metts, and T. D. Bell.

The committee in charge of the Compaign at Sawyerdale are as follows: Woman's Committee, Mrs. E. Rudolph Schoenberg, Chairman, Mesdames, J. S. Boies, B. M. Salley, C. O. Dougherty, B. K. Gleaton, and E. P. Jeffcoat and Misses Blanche Harley, Julia Sawyer, Kittie Knotts, Lennie West, Carrie Gleaton and Nettie Fogle. The Memorial services will be held at 4 P. M., Sunday, October 19th in the Sawyerdale school-house, and will be a joint meeting of all the churches and schools of the district. Mr. W. A. Johnson of North will deliver the Memorial address.

Both of these sections of the county furnished a number of men to the service, and can be proud of the records these boys made. The addresses at both meetings promise to be of the highest character. The subject is one to inspire oratory of the best nature, and the speakers are well fitted to handle it properly. It is the duty of every person who can possibly do so to attend these meetings and render the homage due to the names of these of our own boys who gave their all that freedom and democracy might live.

The program of the meeting at Orangeburg will be announced in the newspapers. Former Judge and Lieut. Colonel Mendel L. Smith will deliver the Memorial address. Music will be rendered by a choir made up from those of the various churches, all the members of which are invited and urged to join the composite choir at this meeting. A fitting program is being arranged, it will all of the chruches will participate.

The school children of the county are proving to be liberal contributors to the fund for erecting a Memorial to the service men of South Carolina. A check has been received from the Orangeburg Schools and one from the Springfield School. The Superintendent of schools at North has written that he has a contribution from the school there which will be sent in later. Doubtless reports of like nature will be received shortly from others of the conuty, the three above being the first to report.

It is suggested by the county chairman of the Memorial Fund Commission that all amounts contributed in the various sections of the county be deposited in the banks of that section and the whole amount sent in at the close of the campaign. A report of such amounts deposited should be made to Mr. Wm. W. Wannamaker, Orangeburg, on Saturday October 25th, so that these amounts may be published so each section may know what the others are doing toward raising the quota alloted.

A Sure Thing.

"Ah always had mo' faith in sympafy dan in congratulations," observed Shinbone. "You knows fo' sure dat dar an't anybody gwinter be jenlous ob you' hahd luck."—Boston Transcript.

"Memorial Services", The Times and Democrat, October 18th, 1919

In this article, the Sawyerdale community held memorial services to honor the fallen soldiers during the World War I at Sawyerdale School. The community furnished men to the service. A memorial fund commission was established to raise funds to erect a memorial to the service men in South Carolina during the war.

Source: https://www.newspapers.com/clip/75036024/memorial-services/

Sawyerdale Memorial Services Last Sunday

Memorial servies were held at Sawyerdale last Sunday the memorial address being made by Mr. W. A. Johnson. The following is the program:

Song—America.

Prayer—C. O. Doughery.

Object of Meeting—H. Rudolph Selvenburg.

Changing of star to Gold—Julia Jones.

While the music of Nearer My God to Thee was beng played by Mrs. C. O. Doughtery the Sawyerdale Service flag was draped in mourning by Misses Mary West, Carrie Gleaton, Lennie West and Julia Sawyer selected because they were sisters of boys who had been in the service.

Address—W. A. Johnson of North S. C.

Presentation of the cut flowers to the family of the departed heroes.

Closing Song, Shall we Gather at the River.

"Sawyerdale Memorial Services Last Sunday", The Times & Democrat, October 24, 1919

In this article, memorial services were held at Sawyerdale to honor fallen soldiers during World War I from the community. A service flag was draped in morning and presentation of the cut flowers to the family of the department heroes.

Source: https://www.newspapers.com/clip/75015532/sawyerdale-memorial-services-last/

Universal Sorrow.

There was deep sorrow at the untimely death of Mr. Sawyer expressed by Governor Manning and the other State officials and the citizens of Columbia generally. The Comptroller General was one of the most popular men in the Capital City, particularly among the social set of which he was a leader. He has made an exceptionally competent State official as is attested by the fact that he was unopposed in the primary of 1915 and again this year.

Carlton Wilkes Sawyer, who succeeded A. W. Jones, chairman of the State tax commission, as Comptroller General, April 1915, as an appointee of Governor Richard I. Manning, was a native of Orangeburg County, having been born at Sawyerdale in that county, 39 years ago. He was the youngest of eight children. His mother was Elizabeth Bamberg, a daughter of Issac Bamberg, former State Treasurer and the late General Francis Marion Bamberg, of Bamberg, who died shortly after his birth. His father, Wilkes Sawyer, then moved the family to the town of Orangeburg in 1889, in order to educate his children. His father served the State throughout the War Between the States as a member of Company A, First South Carolina volunteers, (Hagood's regiment) and following the war, he engaged in farming until his death, in 1888. Carlton W. Sawyer, in 1890, was sent to Columbia where he attended the city graded schools, there remaining for four years, later attending the South Carolina Military Academy, at Charleston, from 1895 to 1898. After leaving the Citadel he kept books for a few months in the Bamberg Cotton Mills, then returning to Columbia where he undertook work for a wholesale firm, later becoming its secretary.

In 1906, a year after the General Assembly passed the corporation license tax, the Comptroller General found it necessary to secure more help in order to carry out the law and Mr. Sawyer was appointed by Comptroller Jones as license clerk, and in 1910 was promoted to chief clerk, the position he held when he was commissioned Comptroller General. His administration, because of his experience as an accountant and his knowledge of the tax problems of the State, caused him to be elected in 1916 and he entered the race unopposed this year.

The deceased took great interest in fraternal organizations, being an Elk, a past chancellor in the Knights of Pythias and a Shriner.

"Universal Sorrrow", The Times and Democrat", April 27, 1918

The obituary of Cartlon W. Sawyer, a Sawyerdale native and son of a Confederate veteran, was appointed and later elected as comptroller general of the state of South Carolina.

Source: https://www.newspapers.com/clip/73678436/universal-sorrow-the-times-and/

FUNERAL LAST SUNDAY

CARLTON SAWYER RECEIVES MAN'S LAST TRIBUTE

Comptroller-General of State Laid to Rest in the Presence of Many Friends and Relatives.

At four-thirty o'clock Sunday afternoon a large crowd of riends and relatives were present at St. Paul's Methodist Church to pay their final tribute of respect to Carlton W. Sawyer, an Orangeburg County boy, who accidentally shot himself at Columbia Friday preceding. The intrement followed the services at the church, and a number of people were present at the burial at Sunnyside.

As comptroller general of South Carolina Mr. Sawyer had lived in Columbia for the past number of years, and quite a large number of Columbia folk came down to attend the funeral. Many State officials, including Governor Manning, were honorary pall bearers. All these officials joined in expressing the universal regret that one so young and promising should prematurely be called away.

The pall bears were as follows:

Active: Joseph L. Nettles, J. S. Odrien, Ashley Tobias, William Glover, W. G. Ellison, H. F. Jackson, R. L. Osborne and W.V. Silverland. Honorary: Governor Richard I. Manning, W. Banks Dove, S. T. Carter, Thomas H. Peeples, W. W. Moore, J. D. Frost, A. W. Jones, William Banks, J. L. Mimnaugh, George L. Baker, J. J. Seibles, D. H. Wise, B. R. Connor, J. Fuller Lyon, T. M. McMichael, A. D. Fair, R. M. Cooper, Sr., T. Q. Boozer, J. J. Cain, Dr. E. C. McGregor, W. G. Smith, J. Pope Matthews, W. H. Gibbs, A. S. Salley, Jr., B. Frank Bamberg, A. W. Summers and M. J. Miller.

The News and Courier Saturday morning carried the following dispatch from Columbia:

Carlton Wilkes Sawyer, comptroller general of South Carolina since April, 1915, accidentally shot himself to death this afternoon about 2:20 o'clock in his room at the residence of Mrs. L. B. McGregor, 1329 Senate street, while cleaning his gun preparatory to going dove hunting tomorrow morning with some of his clerical force. The coroner's jury tonight following an investigation, rendered a verdict that the deceased came to his death accidentally from a gun in his own hands.

Mr. Sawyer is survived by three brothers, W. A. B. Sawyer, of Anniston, Ala; Dr. W. I. Sawyer, of Baltimore, Mr., and S. G. Sawyer, of Baltimore, and four sisters, Mrs. W. C. Wolfe, Mrs. B. B. Barton, Mrs. S. H. Clark and Miss Elizabeth Sawyer all of Orangeburg. The members of the family are expected to arrive in Columbia tonight and tomorrow. It is probable that the funeral services will be held at Orangeburg Sunday morning, stated W. C. Wolfe, brother-in-law of the deceased tonight.

"Funeral Last Sunday", The Times and Democrat", August 27ᵗʰ,1918

In this article, details the circumstances of Carlton Sawyer death which revealed he accidently shot himself and died. His funeral was attended by state dignitaries including Governor Richard Manning.

Source: https://www.newspapers.com/clip/73678222/funeral-last-sunday-the-times-and/

Was Feeling Fine.

Several months ago the Comptroller General had a severe attack of pneumonia, which caused unconsciousness for nearly two weeks. Since that attack he had been in poor health until the past few days when a decided improvement was noted by his friends. This morning and during the early afternoon he told his associates at the State Capitol that he was feeling more fit than in several years past and that he was jubilant; that he did not have to take a vacation to get his strength back. Just before 2 o'clock, after making arrangements with his assistants for some office work they were to accomplish together latter in the day and after communicating with Orangeburg relative to a trip he intended to take there Sunday, he left the State House for his home.

Cleaning Gun.

Reaching the McGregor residence he went into a room across from his own and asked J. C. Whitaker, who was complaining of a headache, how he was feeling. He likewise inquired for some rags to clean his gun. Shortly afterwards Mr. Whitaker said he heard a gun shot in Mr. Sawyer's room and immediately rushed into it. He found Mr. Sawyer lying on his back in front of a "dresser," with his 20-gauge shot gun lying by his right side. He picked up his head, he said, and inquired how the accident happened. Mr. Sawyer gave no recognition and apparently was dead.

He said this happened not later than one-half minute after he heard the shot. The body was lying in a pool of blood and a hole was drilled through the neck, said Mr. Whitaker.

Dr. W. A. Boyd, who reached Mr. Sawyer shortly after the accident, said that apparently the deceased had bled to death from the wound which was a small hole drilled through the center of the neck by No. 6 or 7 birdshot, just above the gase of the collar bone.

There was a dark discoloration around the entrance to the wound, he testified at the coroner's inquest. He said that if Mr Sawyer had committed suicide he took an unusual way to do it, as he had never heard of a case where the victim shot himself through the neck; he usually chooses the temple. He further testified, that in his opinion if the gun had been held to the throat the wound would have been considerably larger and probably would have exploded the gun barrel. Apparently the shot was fired a short distance from the throat, he said.

The theory is that Mr. Sawyer, who apparently was cleaning the gun at that time from the evidence adduced at the inquest, turned over the bottle of oil on the "dresser" and in reaching for it, in some manner, exploded one of the shells in the gun. One of the barrels of the gun was fired and the other contained a loaded shell. On the "dresser," there was a bottle of oil, which he took with him from the State House, according to several of the attaches there who saw him leave with it.

"Funeral Last Sunday", The Times and Democrat, August 27th, 1918 (con't)

FULMER ENDORSED BY HIS NEIGHBORS

To the Voters of Orangeburg County—

We, the undersigned citizens of Orangeburg County, know Mr. H. P. Fulmer to be a successful and energetic farmer and merchant. We have ever found him to be sober and honest, and he enjoys the goodwill and confidence of all the people whom he has had business dealings with for the past years.

He has represented us very ably in the State Legislature for the past four years and we believe he would not only serve the Seventh District with honor in Congress, but he would also conduct himself in such a manner that Orangeburg County would be proud of him. Born and reared in the western part of Orangeburg County and having lived all his life in Orangeburg County, he has ever stood for the best interests of the County and the improvement of the living conditions of its people.

We ask for the voters of old Orangeburg County to stand by Mr. Fulmer, as we feel that he is deserving of their support and of any favors that may be extended to him in the approaching primary. (Signed)

In and Around Norway—P. M. Calvitt, J. D. Steverson, B. T. Garrick, W. N. Gue, B. O. Salley, M. D., Ben Fort, R. M. Davis, J. B. Sutcliffe, A. R. Bates, C. H. Baker, G. F. Gibson, W. J. Moss, J. L. Glover, W. C. Young, W. D. Fogle, J. A. Spires, J. F. Baltzegar, F. S. Gibson, W. J. Bass, Roy Sanford, D. S. Tyler, Jr., Alex C. Phin, Jr., O. W. Morrison, M. D., R. L. Davis, J. A. Price, J. H. Baker, B. G. Rutland, F. F. Bell, D. S. Tyler, Sr. H. E. Garrick, W. W. Fanning, L. E. Davis, M. O. Steverson, J. V. Brown.

Neeses—J. H. Judy, H. E. Baltzegar, J. B. Sheppard, P. C. Hebrard, J. R. Corbett, Jacob T. Williams.

Two Mile Swamp—F. D. Darnell, J. D. Garrick, D. B. Kittrell, W. A. Barrs, J. W. Judy, E. P. Judy, P. H. Jeffcoat, Earle Garrick.

Bolen and Pine Hill—J. H. Berry, D. L. Berry, R. H. Jamison, W. D. Hughes, I. S. Fogle, F. J. Jamison, Rev. Paul W. Hughes, John Gossett.

Livingston—C. G. Glover, J. D. Hutto, L. M. Hair, D. T. Martin.

North—G. K. Livingston, B. H. Salley, L. E. Bell, J. C. Price, J. B. Plunkett, W. L. Whetsone, T. A. Jones, M. D., John T. Jones.

Cope—James F. Boltin, B. B. Boltin, C. S. Gibson, D. W. Bonnette, V. V. Fogle, B. C. Fogle, J. D. Croft, W. M. Ritter, L. E. Spann, D. L. Fogle, H. H. Houck.

Springfield—J. H. Fanning, attorney; E. L. Boland, Mike Gleaton, W. E. Bennett, J. B. Smith, S. J. Holman, J. MacB. Bean, J. C. Porter, H. A. Jumper, J. L. Tyler, S. W. Porter.

Sawyerdale—D. S. Sawyer, C. P. Reed, C. O. Daughterty.

Cordova—M. K. Antley, W. L. Fogle, J. C. Hayden, D. B. Fogle, J. N. Fogle.

(Among these signers, representing all classes of citizenship, farmers, merchants, bankers, and professional men in Orangeburg County, are men who have known H. P. Fulmer all of his life and testify earnestly to his high character, mental capacity and business success, as well as to the interest he takes in his fellow man.)

"Fulmer Endorsed By His Neighbors", Times and Democrat, August 29, 1920

In the article, in 1920, Sawyerdale citizens D.S Sawyer, C.P Reed, and C.O Daughterty joined several citizens of western Orangeburg County endorsed Hampton Pitts Fulmer for Congress. Fulmer, born near Spingfield, South Carolina, who was a successful farmer and merchant in Norway, South Carolina, served in the S.C House of Representatives from 1917-1920. He was elected to Congress in 1920 and served until his death in 1944. During his stint in Congress, he served as chairman of the Agriculture committee.

Source: https://www.newspapers.com/clip/75165927/fulmer-endorsed-by-his-neighbors/

Source: https://history.house.gov/People/Detail/13497

"Jiggs at Home" Will Be Seen at Sawyerdale

SAWYERDALE, April 26.—A play entitled "Jiggs at Home" will be presented in the Sawyerdale school auditorium Fiday night under the direction of the St. George Improvement association, beginning at 8:30 o'clock sharp. Following this there will be a black face minstrel consisting of songs, jokes and recitations. The

"Jiggs at Home Will Be Seen at Sawyerdale", Times and Democrat, April 26, 1921

In this article, a black face minstrel consisting of songs, jokes, and recitations performed at the Sawyerdale School. Black face minstrels perpetuated negative stereotypes of African Americans during the Jim Crow era and was a propaganda tool for Ku Klux Klan to promote racism and justify their pernicious views and acts towards African Americans.

Source: https://www.newspapers.com/clip/74736477/jiggs-at-home-will-be-seen-at/

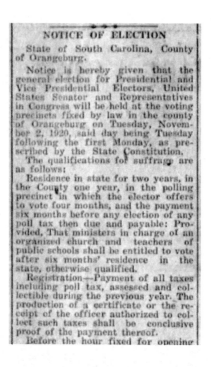

NOTICE OF ELECTION

State of South Carolina, County of Orangeburg.

Notice is hereby given that the general election for Presidential and Vice Presidential Electors, United States Senator and Representatives in Congress will be held at the voting precincts fixed by law in the county of Orangeburg on Tuesday, November 2, 1920, said day being Tuesday following the first Monday, as prescribed by the State Constitution.

The qualifications for suffrage are as follows:

Residence in state for two years, in the County one year, in the polling precinct in which the elector offers to vote four months, and the payment six months before any election of any poll tax then due and payable: Provided, That ministers in charge of an organized church and teachers of public schools shall be entitled to vote after six months' residence in the state, otherwise qualified.

Registration—Payment of all taxes including poll tax, assessed and collectible during the previous year. The production of a certificate or the receipt of the officer authorized to collect such taxes shall be conclusive proof of the payment thereof.

Before the hour fixed for opening

Cauthen, R E Crosland.
Sawyerdale—J. S. Boles, C. O. Dougherty, K. R. Schoenberg.
Springfield

"Notice of Election", The Times and Democrat, October 19th, 1920

In this article, references the infamous poll tax, which begun in 1890 to keep African Americans from voting in southern states. Eligible voters were required to pay their poll tax before they could cast a ballot. A grandfather clause excused some poor Whites from payment if they had an ancestor who voted before the Civil War, but there were no exemptions for African Americans. The Election Managers in the Sawyerdale precinct were J.S. Boles, C.O. Doughtery, and K.R Schoenberg.

In his autobiography, *Up From Slavery,* Booker T. Washington quoted, "I believe that in time, through the operation of intelligence and friendly race relations, all cheating at the ballot box in the South will cease. It will be apparent that the white man who begins by cheating a Negro out of his ballot soon learns to cheat a white man out of his, and that the man who does this ends his career of dishonesty by theft of property or by some equally serious crime. In my opinion, the time will come when the South will encourage all of its citizens to vote.

Source: https://www.newspapers.com/clip/75094125/notice-of-election-the-times-and/

About the Author

Dr. Walter B. Curry, Jr. is a native of Orangeburg, South Carolina. He received a bachelor's degree in political science from South Carolina State University and has earned several graduate degrees in education, which includes a doctorate degree in Curriculum and Instruction from Argosy University, Sarasota.

In 2018, Dr. Curry launched Renaissance Publications, LLC. On September 1, 2018, he published his first genealogy book, The Thompson Family: Untold Stories from the Past (1830-1960). The book chronicles the reflections and experiences of his relatives that shed new light on African American history in Aiken County and South Carolina. Several narratives include a slave who purchased his freedom, a relative who served as a cook in the Confederate Army, a young relative who was tragically murdered, and a sharecropper who became a prominent soil conservationist. In October 2019, Dr. Curry received the 2019 African American Historical and Genealogy Society Book Award in the nonfiction category genealogy for his book. On February 12, 2020, the South Carolina Legislature recognized him for his significant work in service to African American history and heritage in South Carolina and congratulated him on his book award. In addition, Dr. Curry was selected for the South Carolina State University 40 Under 40 Inaugural Class for his professional accomplishments and dedication to the university.

Dr. Curry is a member of several civic, historical, and professional organizations, which include South Carolina Genealogical Society, Orangeburg County Historical Society, Aiken-Barnwell Genealogical Society, and the African American Historical and Genealogical Society. He is also a volunteer for the International African American Museum. As a volunteer, he coordinates outreach efforts to local stakeholders to solicit memberships and partnerships.

In addition, Dr. Curry has done several book signings and presentations at local conferences, workshops, bookstores, museums, and schools across the state and nationwide. His most recent project is "Salley and The Thompson Family," an exhibit in the Aiken County Historical Museum that featured the founding of Salley, South Carolina and the illumination of his ancestors' and relatives' stories through artifacts and primary sources.

Dr. Curry currently lives in Columbia, South Carolina with his wife, Takiyah S. Curry, who is a registered nurse and graduate of the University of South Carolina. They have two sons, Braxton and Braylon.

ACKNOWLEDGEMENTS

This section of the book acknowledges family members, individuals, and ancillary organizations who contributed to the contents of this book and continuous inspiration for the completion of the book.

Seawright-Ellison Family Members

Cheryl Seawright Curry
Robert L. Seawright
Arthur L. Seawright
Stephanie Seawright Smith
Connie Seawright
Sharon Seawright Childs
Alvin, Michael, and Cecil Ellison
Martha Ellison Oliver
Gregory Garvin
Barbra Seawright Allen
Nancy Johnson Seawright
Andrea S. Roulac
Francis Williams
Lessie & Randy Mccollough
Tonja Rachell Seawright

Individuals

Sam Williams, Member of the group formerly known as "Tommy Ellison & Five Singing Stars"

Katina Williams, Businessowner & Local Artist

Bobby Donaldson, Ph. D, Associate Professor of History, University of South Carolina

Toni Carrier, Director of the Center for Family History, International African American Museum

Wayne O'Bryant, Local African American Author & Historian

Cynthia Hardy, Director of the Wagener Museum

Gregory Harris, African American Salley Family Historian

Nicholas Drayton, United States Army Sergeant and Businessman

Rev. Lester Smalls, Member of Martha Schofield High School Alumni Association

Tonya B. Guy, Historian of the Old Edgefield District Genealogical Society

Janet Corbett, Historian of the Corbett family

Harry Govan, President of Harry Govan Gospel Song Ministries

Willie Anderson, Member of the Palmetto State Barber Association

Steve Tuttle, Archivist at the S.C Department of Archives & History

Rev. Haskell Staley, Pastor of Friendship Baptist Church

John Staley, Son of Paul & Ella Holmes Staley

Deborah Harmon, Historian & Archivist of the Gregg-Graniteville Library

Carol Mciver, Historian of the Phillips family

Maggie Staley Tucker, daughter of Lester and Mrytis Wooden Staley, Sr.

The Honorable Ladonna Hall, Mayor of Salley, South Carolina

Eric Powell, Director of the Orangeburg County Historical Society

Bob Cothran, Owner of Meeting on Main Restaurant

Organizations

Palmetto State Barber Association

Friends of Rocky Swamp United Methodist Church

The South Carolina Historical Society

The Aiken-Barnwell Genealogical Society

Orangeburg County Historical Society

Antioch Missionary Baptist Church

The Carolina Panaroma

Smyrna Missionary Baptist Church
Baughmanville Missionary Baptist Church
The Aiken County Historical Museum
The Ellison-Miles Family Council
The South Carolina Department of Archives & History
Martha Schofield High School Alumni Association
Fountain Inn Museum

Book Cover Design
Verlene Little, Founder of Onyx Print Design Solutions

Book Editing &Publishing
Palmetto Publishing